ADVANCE PRAISE FOR

Beyond Me, My Selfie, and I

"In an increasingly narcissistic culture, Teresa Tomeo throws readers a lifeline. With her typical cleverness and depth, she reminds us why 'it is not all about you'...but us! Drop the selfie stick and pick up this book."

—Raymond Arroyo, *New York Times* bestselling author and EWTN News managing editor and founding news director

"Teresa Tomeo felt the cultural pulse and has detected a serious heart ailment—narcissistic self-love. From one symptom (overindulging in taking selfies), she proceeds to identify many others: obsessive-compulsive Internet and media addictions, isolation from actual human contact, loss of God and a resultant loss of meaning. Yet Tomeo is also wise enough to suggest healing prescriptions. Read this book and discover how you, too, can love God and other people in order to get out of a profoundly self-centered downward spiral and break free to authentic joy and peace."

—Fr. Mitch Pacwa, SJ, biblical scholar, EWTN host, and president and founder of Ignatius Productions

"Teresa Tomeo takes a clear picture of our technologically obsessed, self-absorbed culture. She presents a compelling case: The closer you are to yourself, the farther you are from God. *Me, My Selfie & I* gives a true picture of reality."

—Dr. Ray Guarendi, clinical psychologist, nationally syndicated talk radio and television host and author, *Discipline That Lasts a Lifetime*

"Teresa Tomeo skillfully lays out one of the most powerful yet counterintuitive truths of the human experience: that focusing on yourself won't lead to happiness. Our self-obsessed culture needs this message now more than ever."

—Jennifer Fulwiler, host of "The Jennifer Fulwiler Show" (SiriusXM) and bestselling author, *Something Other Than God*

"As the wand of Narcissis (aka the selfie stick) waves across our world, spreading egotism and selfishness, Teresa Tomeo gives us a clear picture of what the 'selfie age' is doing to our society. *Beyond Me, My Selfie & I* offers us a better way of living and growing closer to Christ. Do yourself a favor: Put down your smart phone and pick up this book. You'll be surprised what you have been missing!"

—Michele Faehnle, coauthor, *Divine Mercy for Moms*

"It is difficult to imagine that the culture of narcissism has moved to hyper-narcissism. Yet this seems to be the interior and virtual world in which so many young people live—with new generations clamoring to join them.... Not content to leave the culture, and its vulnerable youth, to the darkness of egocentric isolation, Tomeo uses Scripture, philosophy, common sense, and prayer to reintroduce light and love into the emptiness and alienation of our time. She incites us to move beyond the reduction of ourselves to mere images and facades pandering for attention—and to follow the call and grace of Christ to rise to love and faith—and so to embrace our *true* nature, dignity, and destiny."

—Fr. Robert J. Spitzer, SJ, PhD, author, *Finding True Happiness* and president of the Magis Center of Reason and Faith

"When I heard Teresa Tomeo was writing a book about me, I was thrilled! Then I realized it wasn't written just about me. It's written about all of us who live in this 'me' centered world. As always, Teresa helps us be less self-centered and more God-centered. I may even take a selfie with this book to share it with others!

—Lino Rulli, The Catholic Guy on SiriusXM Satellite Radio

"In *Beyond Me, My Selfie & I,* Teresa Tomeo has once again shown herself to be one of the most insightful, readable media critics in our society today. In this brilliant analysis of the "selfie" phenomenon, she exposes "me, myself, and I" as the false path to happiness that it really is, and asks her readers thought-provoking questions that will help them find the road to true joy. Everyone with a smart phone should read this book—and share it with their friends!"

—Sue Ellen Browder, author, *Subverted: How I Helped the Sexual Revolution Hijack the Women's Movement*

Beyond Me, My Selfie & I

•••••••

Finding REAL HAPPINESS in a Self-Absorbed World

•••••••

Teresa Tomeo

AN IMPRINT OF
FRANCISCAN MEDIA
Cincinnati, Ohio

Cover and book design by Mark Sullivan

Library of Congress Cataloging-in-Publication Data
Names: Tomeo, Teresa, author.
Title: Beyond me, my selfie, and I : finding real happiness in a self-absorbed world / Teresa Tomeo.
Description: Cincinnati : Servant, 2016. | Includes bibliographical references and index.
Identifiers: LCCN 2016026177 | ISBN 9781632530462 (trade paper : alk. paper)
Subjects: LCSH: Happiness—Religious aspects—Catholic Church. | Christianity and culture. | Christian life—Catholic authors. | Catholic Church—Doctrines.
Classification: LCC BV4647.J68 T66 2016 | DDC 248.4—dc23
LC record available at https://lccn.loc.gov/2016026177

ISBN 978-1-63253-046-2

Published by Servant
an imprint of Franciscan Media
28 W. Liberty St.
Cincinnati, OH 45202
www.FranciscanMedia.org

Printed in the United States of America.
Printed on acid-free paper.
16 17 18 19 20 5 4 3 2 1

—CONTENTS—

—INTRODUCTION—

"Time for Another Selfie." These words stopped me in my tracks as I was wandering through the aisles of my local Bed Bath & Beyond. They were painted on a piece of colorful canvas, sold as wall art in the home décor section. Dozens of other customers walked by the framed piece, not noticing it; their lack of interest seemed to me to be just one more sign that selfies have become engrained in our culture, our way of thinking, our way of living.

That quote may seem innocent enough to some—just a cute and very up-to-date expression to hang in a young person's college dorm room or new apartment. It's anything but that, however. And as I stood there with my mouth open, staring at the frame, I thought about what a statement it made—and not a very good one. After all, I have a hard enough time being selfless and not getting caught up in my own heart's desires as well as everyday concerns, and I am a person with a pretty strong faith. I also have a built-in accountability system with a network of solid Christian friends, coworkers, and family. So if believers like me still struggle with regularly trying to "decrease so God can increase," as St. John the Baptist reminds us, how much more difficult is it for nonbelievers and fallen-away Catholics (whose numbers happen to be increasing steadily)?

Selfies, of course, aren't the root cause of the many problems in our lives and our society. I'm sure you'll agree, however, that pride and selfishness certainly rank pretty high up there in the trouble-causing category. Selfies are a by-product of a world that has come to place autonomy, personal satisfaction, and instant gratification above all else.

Let's imagine a young, impressionable person seeing "Time for Another Selfie" several times a day. Doesn't it reinforce an "It's all about me" attitude? That so-called home décor, along with some other selfie-related incidents that have occurred in my work and travels recently, got me thinking about the reason for and the fall-out from the world's fascination—and my own fascination, quite frankly—with capturing just about every day-to-day activity and posting, tweeting, and pinning it for all the world to see.

As a media person who is often in the spotlight, I recognize the importance of keeping websites and social media pages interesting, up to date, and even personal on some level. It's all about connecting with people, or so we've convinced ourselves. However, given the growing focus on instant personal gratification, I'm wondering if the "selfie syndrome" is a sign of something much deeper...and more troubling.

Could it be that our obsession with technology reveals a weakening, and in some cases even a rejection, of what it means to be Christian? What impact do those tech ties have on one's own faith? What impact is it having on family relationships and friendships? Even though I write and speak about media influence regularly, my husband has noticed that, at times—when we're in the car, for example—I am paying more attention to my phone than to him. What does that say about what is most important to me?

As believers we are called to lay down our lives for God and each other. Christianity is all about going beyond ourselves in order to live a new, more fulfilling life on earth, make a difference in the lives of others, and culminate (God willing) with an eternity in heaven. If we're preoccupied with self, there is little room for true *JOY*—as in, *J*esus first, *O*thers second, and *Y*ourself last.

An increasing amount of research shows how greatly we are impacted by our media- and selfie-saturated culture. If the tech-obsessed culture is affecting the life of a Catholic talk show host and media expert, what about the average person out there who isn't familiar with God? As I pondered this question, I began to notice the obsession with selfies more and more. And as I continued researching this topic, it was clear that I wasn't the only one worried about where the selfie trend is taking us.

There is now a large body of evidence (not to mention plenty of shocking headlines) showing the connection between selfie obsession and a number of societal ills. Christian thinkers, theologians, and religious leaders are weighing in about how this obsession negatively plays itself out in our homes, parishes, and communities. In a nutshell, selfies are not exactly causing us to engage in self-reflection (no pun intended) on the things that really matter in life—faith, family, and service to others. Instead selfies seem to be having the opposite effect. They're causing more of us to believe the world actually does revolve around us, and they're keeping us stuck at the surface, leading us to focus only on worldly matters.

By writing this book I am hoping to help us all go deeper. In each chapter we will examine a current issue, or vice; a corresponding antidote, or virtue; and an example of someone who can help us break a particular aspect of the selfie syndrome. To help you get your bearings, I've included a little quiz so you can discern whether this particular issue is a problem area for you. If so, don't worry—we're all in this together! Just take a deep breath, and let's explore how we can grow in this area of our lives. I'll also give you some prompts for reflection and self-examination, which will help you go beyond yourself, look around at a world in need, and ultimately look up toward God, the only source of true happiness. My hope is that the research, real-life experiences, practical resources, and last (but certainly not least) what our Catholic faith has to say about our current culture will not only help us reverse a disturbing trend but also remind us where true and lasting joy really comes from.

—CHAPTER ONE—

Picture This

An Eye-Opening Scene from Our Selfie-Obsessed Culture

> The world of communications can help us either to expand our knowledge or to lose our bearings.
>
> —Pope Francis, Forty-Eighth World Communications Day (June 1, 2014)

Whether you refer to them as "aha moments" or "wake-up calls," I've had several such major insights, and they inspired me to write this book. One of the most profound occurred on a recent trip to Italy. This particular wake-up call came in 2015 while my husband, Dominick, and I were cohosting a pilgrimage for the Shroud of Turin exhibit. Dominick and I are both Italian American, so Italy is our favorite place to visit, and we always try to work in a few days to ourselves before and after each pilgrimage to take in the breathtaking beauty of what I call "the motherland."

This time we landed in Milan, so we decided to vacation in northern Italy's Lake District, comprised of Lakes Como, Maggiore, and Garda. We had already visited Lake Como and had heard a great deal about the wonderful treasures of Lake Garda, so once we landed in Milan, off we went to our quaint little hotel situated between the stunning southern lakeside towns of Desenzano and Sirmione. Often travel websites greatly exaggerate the qualities of a particular area in order to gain more clients and make more money, but in the case of Lake Garda, they didn't even do it justice.

Italy is truly the way my husband and I reconnect with our physical and—more important—our spiritual roots. It's wonderful to be proud of our ethnic heritage, but it's even more important to recognize and appreciate being a child of such an incredibly grand and magnificent God.

We had four nights to spend on the banks of this majestic body of water before we were to meet up with the pilgrims in Turin, so we decided to hit a few key spots that would give us an overview of the area, the people, the lifestyle, and the scenery. The Monte Baldo cable-car ride leaving from the little village of Melcesine tucked into the hills along the lake's northeastern shore was at the top of our to-do list.

The twenty-minute cable-car ride climbs 1,700 meters to the top of Mount Baldo, located in the Italian Alps. Thanks to the snowcapped mountains, the blue-green water, and the terra-cotta rooftops in the towns below, we felt like we were about to step into our own version of *The Sound of Music*. Even though the Von Trapp clan was from Austria, we couldn't help but feel as if Julie Andrews (playing Maria von Trapp) was going to greet us when we reached the summit. It was a little slice of heaven on earth.

To top it off, this cableway has a unique feature that makes the experience even more enjoyable. The car actually slowly revolves, providing a 360-degree bird's-eye view. It truly is awe-inspiring.

Well, at least it was for us. I don't know about the young couple that was among those on the cable ride with us. From the minute these two lovebirds stepped onto the platform, for them it was all about shooting selfies. All right, already—we can certainly understand one or two selfies, given the backdrop. But nonstop selfies, one after the other, on the platform, in the crowded cable car, at the top of one of the most majestic mountains in Northern Italy, and all the way back down again is not just a bit much, it's ridiculous.

Sure, Dominick and I took our share of photos with our cell phones. Who wouldn't? But we did spend most of the experience trying to soak up the sights with our own eyes as we soared into the Italian Alps. It seemed the only time this couple put their phones down was to step on and off the cable car. The rest was spent posing, giggling, and snapping away. If they weren't taking selfies, they were reviewing them over and over again, pointing, nodding, and high-fiving each other as they went through their endless selfie stockpile. They were utterly oblivious to everyone and everything around them. The only thing that mattered was what was on the small screens in their hands.

That's why, thanks to this experience and others like it, I found Pope Francis's words—regarding communications either causing us to gain knowledge or lose our bearings—to be both profound and prophetic, helping us to stop to think about just how lost in the high-tech, self-absorbed world we've become.

- Men and women undergoing drastic cosmetic surgery because they're unhappy with the way they look in pictures.
- One young person actually attempted suicide because of an unflattering selfie posted on Facebook.[1]
- Tourists risking great bodily harm and worse just to capture the perfect self-image on their phone to post, tweet, and text their friends, family, and anyone else who will help give them their fifteen minutes of fame.

Lost on the Digital Highway

We have lost our bearings. Even if our selfie experiences haven't been as dramatic as some in recent headlines, our obsession with selfies, smartphones, and the virtual world in general can distract us from the spiritual practices that are crucial in our search for true happiness. We need to have the ability to look upward and outward, ponder and reflect, as the Blessed Mother did so often. As Pope Francis stated in his message for the forty-eighth World Communications Day on June 1, 2014, if we're not careful, the digital highway can become a dead-end street:

> It is not enough to be passersby on the digital highways, simply "connected"; connections need to grow into true encounters. We cannot live apart, closed in on ourselves. We need to love and to be loved. We need tenderness.

We can be so much more than just passersby "on a digital highway," as Pope Francis says, if we choose to use media—and in this case primarily social media—for more than just a vehicle to attract attention to ourselves. Maybe instead of posting one more selfie, we instead pass along an announcement about a fund-raiser for a local charity. Perhaps there is someone in your circle of friends who is suffering and in need of prayers or some other type of support. Posting a request for prayers can have huge results; it's a way to pay it forward, as the saying goes. This is the love and tenderness to which the pope is referring.

Quiz Time: Have You Caught the Selfie Syndrome?

Let's find out. Do you recognize yourself in any of these situations?

1. Christmas is just around the corner! Which of these is most likely one of your special memories?

   a. Putting reindeer antlers on the dog...and posting it on Facebook.

   b. Capturing the excitement of the children's faces as they open gifts on your cell...and texting them to Grandma and Grandpa.

   c. Throwing your husband's laptop out the window so you both can "sleep in heavenly peace."

2. In the good old summertime, where are you most likely to be found?

   a. Hiking or biking with your kids through a local park, each of you blocking the sounds of nature with earbuds blasting your own personal sound track.

   b. Avoiding the pool like the plague, worried about the world catching sight of you in a bathing suit.

   c. Packing a picnic hamper...while posting delectable snapshots on Pinterest.

3. It's your anniversary! Your husband presents you with the ultimate gift: a week away on a remote island, just the two of you. What's the first thought that pops into your head?

   a. What'll we do with the kids?

   b. Does that cute little swimsuit I haven't worn for three years still fit?

   c. Do they have wi-fi?

Do any of these scenes sound remotely familiar? Most of us don't think of ourselves as selfie- or self-obsessed, but if you're honest in answering the above questions, you'll probably realize, as I did, that we have all caught the selfie syndrome to some extent. OK, so taking festive photos of Fido and your family and posting them faster than you can say, "Pass the hot chocolate," is not necessarily a sign that you've gone completely overboard in the selfie craze category. But my hope is that the questions will help you stop to think the next time you're about to pick up that cell phone. Is it really necessary to tell the whole world what we're doing at any given moment?

"It's All about You" vs. Walking Humbly with God

St. Teresa of Avila (my namesake!) used to teach that the best way to root out a deeply entrenched vice is to practice the corresponding virtue. It's a good idea to take our cues from the saints in Scripture and tradition, and to learn from their lives and writings as we make our way in the Christian life.

When you think about it, the word *ego* could be an acronym that stands for "Easing God Out." That's exactly what self-centered people do because they are engrossed solely in themselves, concerned only with their own needs, interests, and welfare.

The best way to fight this self-centeredness, of course, is by cultivating the virtue of humility, which is the opposite of self-centeredness. Humility helps us keep our ego in check by recognizing our faults, shortcomings, and our constant need for the mercy and love of God. Humility reminds us that there is a God and it's not us.

The Woman at the Well

In John 4:1–26, we read the story of Jesus meeting a Samaritan woman at the well. This woman provides us with a great example of humility. Deep down she knew she was living a sinful life, but she was still willing and open to hear what Jesus had to say about her search for happiness, which had so far left her empty.

Does this resonate with you? Do you ever catch yourself in a moment of supreme self-centeredness and suddenly realize that what you need most is a good serving of humble pie? Don't be afraid to bring this to the light...perhaps even in the sacrament of reconciliation. Jesus didn't reject the woman at the well—he revealed to her everything she had ever done, and loved her anyway. In the same way, you can bring your most embarrassing, self-centered thoughts to him and know that he will strengthen you to try again.

Why is it important to recognize and root out the tendency toward self-centeredness and cultivate humility? Catholic evangelist, author, and international speaker Matthew Kelly says the way we see the world is the way we live our lives. Whether it's at Christmas time, on vacation, or in our day-to-day lives, if we're continually spending a good chunk of our time integrating some piece of technology into everything we do, then Houston, we have a problem. Looking at the images of ourselves on our phones, on Facebook, or incessantly tweeting what we had for lunch or what we're wearing to the party means our world isn't going to go much further than me, my selfie, and I. And this is a very skewed, very limited view.

How often, for example, have we seen pictures of pilgrims gathered in St. Peter's Square struggling to get some sort of a selfie shot near or with the pope? Instead of enjoying the spiritual experience of being at a papal Mass or audience, they spend their time trying to insert themselves into the picture, quite literally missing the real meaning of the event.

For Dominick and me, that cable ride was a mini retreat, a private little pilgrimage. God's by no means through with us yet, but because we spent so many years oblivious to God and his creation, we now try to be more acutely aware of the grandeur all around us, expressed so beautifully in the book of Psalms:

> When I look at your heavens, the work of your fingers,
> the moon and the stars which you have established,
> what are human beings that you are mindful of them,
> mortals that you care for them? (8:3–4)

It's worth thinking about, isn't it? How many times do we fail to recognize God in the world around us, thanking him for the creativity and intelligence within us? How often do we praise and thank him for making us in his glorious image and likeness, and for the marvelous beauty of his creation, the "work of his fingers"?

And how often are we more like the couple on the cable car, oblivious to everything but ourselves? What does it take for God to get our attention, like the Samaritan woman in John's Gospel who came to the well in the middle of the day? As she approached the well to draw water, she had no earbuds or smartphone to distract her; she could hear the Lord speak to her very clearly: "Give me a drink" (John 4:7).

Imagine what she must have thought of this strange man who had broken into her reality, talking to *her*. What was more, he said the most extraordinary things—he offered her *living water!* And somehow (she wasn't sure quite how) he knew all about her. "You are right in saying, 'I have no husband'; for you have had five husbands, and he whom you now have is not your husband" (John 4:17–18).

Jesus wasn't saying these things to be cruel. He wanted to shake her up, to get her attention, to make her truly see herself for the first time the way *God* saw her.

He wanted her to know that she was made for something more. He wanted her to recognize just how valuable she was in his eyes. She was born to witness to the truth. And she saw! A new awareness began to seep into her consciousness. "Come and see a man who told me everything I have ever done! He cannot be the Messiah, can he?" (John 4:29).

And so it is with us. In a way, selfies—like every other aspect of social media—are not intrinsically evil. They are a form of communication; tools we can use to share what is important to us. Selfies are popular because they are meant to be shared among friends and then more friends. It's that old Faberge shampoo TV commercial on steroids: "You tell two friends... and they'll tell two friends...and so on, and so on, and so on."

However, for many people, using social media has turned into a compulsion. One study released by Baylor University in 2014 showed that 60 percent of college students admit they're addicted to their cell phones, with most of that time spent on Instagram, Snapchat, and Twitter.[2] Another study from Baylor estimated that female college students use their cell phones as much as ten hours a day, and eight hours for male students.[3]

That same study reported that many participants experienced a great deal of anxiety when separated from their phones for seventy-five minutes. Spending as much time on our phones as we do at a full-time job can impact our relationships, our choices, and our view of the world, as Pope Benedict XVI highlighted back in 2011.

> The new technologies allow people to meet each other beyond the confines of space and of their own culture, creating in this way an entirely new world of potential friendships. This is a great opportunity, but it also requires greater attention to and awareness of possible risks.[4]

Benedict warned that we can easily lose our perspective when we focus on ourselves. If we view the world based only our needs or interests, we create a "virtual reality" that becomes increasingly distanced from the real world and the needs of others.

> Who is my "neighbor" in this new world? Does the danger exist that we may be less present to those whom we encounter in our everyday life? Is there is a risk of being more distracted because our attention is fragmented and absorbed in a world "other" than the one in which we live? Do we have time to reflect critically on our choices and to foster human relationships which are truly deep and lasting? It is important always to remember that virtual contact cannot and must not take the place of direct human contact with people at every level of our lives.[5]

As we'll explore in this book, whether it's Italy, Ireland, or Idaho, it's important to take time to appreciate the glory all around us, and to approach life ready to experience it all unfettered by the need to plop ourselves and our wants in the middle of every single frame. If we don't put down the camera and aspire to something better, we'll soon suffer the consequences of a selfie-centered cable car ride to nowhere.

The Samaritan woman, for example, is known as one of the first evangelists. Soon after her encounter with Christ, she left her water jug behind and went into town to tell the people about Jesus—the same people she was trying to avoid in the first place. Think about that for a minute. She came to the well at high noon in the scorching heat because she wanted to steer clear of the crowds and the stares. Everyone else would be inside at that time of day, so she could do what she needed to do and get back to her life. She was living in isolation, closed in on herself. Once she discovered who she really was in Christ, everything changed—not only for her but for the people to whom she witnessed.

Put Down the Phone and Be a Positive Influence

The story of the woman at the well demonstrates how one person making a change can have a far-reaching and long-lasting impact. Never underestimate how your own actions might positively influence your circle of family and friends. Here are a few suggestions to help yourself and those you care about be more than just passersby on the digital highway.

- Invite some friends over for a phone-free get-together; kindly insist that if they do bring their phones with them, they leave them turned off. Build your time together around great conversation, food, wine, and maybe a fun game or two, with no one allowed to check e-mails or texts. You'd be surprised how much fun live interaction can be. (Recently there was actually a series of public service announcements on TV encouraging just that. It's hard to believe it's gotten to the point where we need to see actors have a great time just being together and talking face-to-face sans phones, but it's a catchy campaign with an important message.)[6] Who knows, you might start a new and positive trend!

• If you're a parent, encourage phone-free family time. Author, speaker, and pediatrician Dr. Meg Meeker, a frequent guest on my radio show, made this a daily rule in her house. After school the cell phones went in a basket on the kitchen counter and could not be retrieved or used until the kids were heading out to school the next morning.

• Family meals should be a definite phone-free time slot—and not only while everyone is sitting around the table eating. How about encouraging your children to help with meal preparation, making it another family activity? You might get some push back at first, but eventually the kids will come to cherish that special time together. Despite what you may think, children still look to their parents for guidance, encouragement, and yes, discipline.

• During Lent or Advent commit to fasting from social media one day a week with the intention of incorporating more quiet time and more prayer time in your life for the long term.

• Use the time you would have spent taking and posting selfies for Scripture reading, journaling, or listening quietly to what God might be trying to say to you.

• Make a serious effort to spend time in silence in front of the Blessed Sacrament. Eucharistic Adoration might feel intimidating at first and frustrating at times because our minds tend to wander. St. Teresa of Avila, a great mystic and doctor of the Church, struggled with concentration in prayer, so don't worry—you're in good company. But just get to the chapel and listen; listen to God and listen to the beautiful peace and quiet.

• After incorporating one or more of these suggestions, reflect upon the impact the added quiet has had on your life, your outlook, and your relationships, especially your relationship with God.

In order to find what we're truly searching for, we need to first find out who we really are. This begins with discovering—or rediscovering—God. But how does this happen in a world that doesn't recognize God anymore, a world where people live apart, wrapped up in themselves and their technology? This book is an attempt to address, examine, and I hope, answer this question. It's one that has been nagging me for some time.

If we are willing to silence ourselves and our phones and share the truths we discover about who we are in God's eyes, we can become powerful witnesses to the truth. The choice is yours.

Come to the Quiet

Putting down the gadgets and stepping away from technology in order to spend time enjoying, contemplating, and reflecting more on your surroundings is not just something to do with your spare time. Rather, as many of our great saints have shown us, it's an essential component of a healthier and more balanced life.

Read through these quotes and pick your favorite. Post it on your bathroom mirror to reflect upon each morning.

> It's best to learn to silence the faculties and to cause them to be still so that God may speak. (St. John of the Cross)

> God speaks in the silence of the heart. Listening is the beginning of prayer. (St. Teresa of Calcutta)

> Patience, prayer and silence. These are what give strength to the soul. (St. Faustina)

For Christians, "coming to the quiet" is absolutely essential if we don't want to spend our lives going around in circles. Constantly putting our own needs and desires first through the endless pursuit of "me-focused" media messaging and self-gratification—twenty-four hours a day, seven days a week—is a one-way ticket to unbridled unhappiness.

Pope Francis tells us: "We are challenged to be people of depth, attentive to what is happening around us and spiritually alert."[7]

So, the next time you find yourself caught up the selfie craze, take some time to cultivate a clear-eyed attentiveness to the world around you. See with fresh eyes both its natural beauty and the people right in front of you, just waiting for a bit of personal connection.

Time for Self-Reflection

- Spend a few minutes with this verse from the Gospel of St. Luke:

> But Mary treasured all these words and pondered them in her heart. (Luke 2:19)

- What do the words *treasured* and *pondered* mean to you?
- When was the last time you *pondered* an experience in your life?

—CHAPTER TWO—

Where the Selfie Sticks

The Selfie Scene in Numbers

Our vanity is the constant enemy of our dignity.[8]

—Anne Sophie Swetchine

The selfie craze has led to the creation of completely new product lines. You've probably heard of the selfie stick. It's an elongated rod that attaches to a cell phone or camera, enabling you to take your selfie from a variety of different angles.

In the summer of 2015, the California Screamin' roller coaster at Disney California's Adventure Park was shut down for over an hour in the middle of the ride because one of the passengers thought pulling out his selfie stick to get that precious shot was a great idea. His stunt was a breach of the park's safety policies, and it led to an emergency evacuation when he refused to put the device away. While Adventure Park doesn't ban selfie sticks (yet), the devices pose a real risk because of the potential danger of someone getting struck and injured by a flying projectile when the ride is going at top speeds. To most of us, this would seem to be common sense...and yet, believe it or not, theme park employees still have to remind visitors to keep the sticks tucked away while on the rides.[9]

This self-absorbed insistence on the indiscriminate use of selfie sticks has caused so many headaches and safety concerns that the sticks have been banned in a variety of places, including the ancient Colosseum in Rome, the Palace of Versailles in France, and the National Gallery in London. And the list keeps growing. It's not the selfies and the selfie sticks that are the problem; it's the way people allow themselves to be influenced, or in some cases controlled, by these items through their actions. It's the selfish preoccupation of the person who uses them.

In this chapter, we're going to take a closer look at the selfie stick aspect of the selfie syndrome: the drive for adventure, even risky adventure—particularly when we seek it out at the expense of others in a way that is rude or even dangerous. This is an appropriate description of the actions of those going overboard when trying to grab the perfect selfie. We'll take a closer look at some real-life stories and the fallout that often results from life-threatening behavior that stems from thinking only of "me, myself, and I."

By way of contrast, we'll also explore two virtuous antidotes to this kind of behavior: generosity and kindness. If the man on the roller coaster, for example, would have thought about the other riders and the park employees, so much trouble, expense, and risk could have been avoided. It was a selfish act that cost money, time, and the possible endangerment of others. The kind and generous thing to do would have been to keep his arms, legs, and selfie stick inside the roller coaster car at all times.

We'll look at the powerful witness of the woman in the Gospel who was healed by touching the hem of Jesus's garment (see Mark 5:25–35). Given the dire health situation of this hemorrhaging woman, who could have blamed her if she made a scene as Jesus was walking through town? She had been subject to bleeding for twelve years, and despite countless visits to one physician after the next, nothing had changed. But in addition to having faith, she was also kind and considerate of the throngs of people trying to get close to Jesus. Instead of making a scene, she made a small gesture—she reached out and simply touched Jesus's garment. That's all it took—she was healed. She helped herself while still being conscious of others around her who also might be in need of healing, whether physical or spiritual.

But first, you know what's coming—it's Quiz Time!

Quiz Time: Do You Have the Selfie-Stick Syndrome?

Ask yourself the following questions to see if you allow your preoccupation with technology to override good judgment at times.

1. The last time you were at a wedding, did you...
   a. Get teary-eyed as you watched the groom's eyes light up at the sight of his bride?
   b. Shoulder-block the videographer as you jockeyed for the best shot of the best man's toast?
   c. Get the wedding party and yourself banned from the Holiday Inn for life for taking risqué candid shots in the lobby fountain?
2. You chaperoned your kid's last field trip and are now banned from participating in any more school activities because you...
   a. Encouraged your group to clamber up the T-Rex skeleton in the Natural History Museum and posted incriminating evidence on the school Facebook page.
   b. Took your group on a six-mile detour up the Appalachian Trail when you couldn't read the trail signs at the local park without your GPS.
   c. Confiscated the kids' cell phones and tossed them out the bus window, cracking the principal's windshield in the process.

3. At your last high school reunion, you were voted the alumnus most likely to...

   a. Be featured in a Lifetime movie.
   b. Die at the hands of an aggressive bodyguard mistaking you for paparazzi.
   c. Go Amish.

Rude and Risky vs. Kind and Generous

The selfie syndrome has become so commonplace that we don't even notice it anymore...and that's a big part of the issue. That couple on the cable car ride along with the nonchalant attitude of dozens of tourists with us that fateful afternoon in Italy's Lake District are no longer exceptions in our world but our new normal. And as stunned as my husband and I were by the couple we observed on our Italian Alps cable car ride, their actions pale in comparison to other selfie fanatics.

The "I am all that and a bag of chips" attitude has become so insidious that we are witnessing one selfie-connected catastrophe after the next. Shocking cases grab the headlines and our attention briefly: People so determined to post, tweet, and text one more picture of themselves that they take all kinds of chances with their safety (and their sanity). Society still tends to treat these cases as rarities. And yet these stories are not only commonplace but an outward example of a much deeper issue. Sometimes the problem is not that they think too highly of themselves...but do not value themselves enough. Meet Danny Bowman. He is the self-described former selfie addict from Great Britain. According to an interview published in London's *Daily Mirror* newspaper, Danny's obsession kept him from the outside world and eventually landed him in a mental health facility.

Nineteen-year-old Danny Bowman spent hours each day taking selfies on his iPhone, sometimes as many as two hundred images a day. In his vain attempt to find the perfect self-portrait, he dropped almost thirty pounds and became severely depressed, ultimately winding up in the hospital due to a drug overdose.

> I was constantly in search of taking the perfect selfie and when I realized I couldn't, I wanted to die. I lost my friends, my education, my health and almost my life. He started posting selfies to Facebook at the age of 15, but found his addiction spiraling out of control after his aspirations of being a male model were dashed by a rejection at a casting session for an agency in 2011. It was the beginning of a two-year addiction that culminated in his suicide attempt.

Danny insists his situation, as desperate and bizarre as it was, is not all that unusual and can happen to anyone.

> People don't realize when they post a picture of themselves on Facebook or Twitter it can so quickly spiral out of control. It becomes a mission to get approval and it can destroy anyone. It's a real problem like drugs, alcohol or gambling. I don't want anyone to go through what I've been through.[10]

Due to the number of people putting themselves in harm's way just to take a selfie, 2014 became known as the "year of the death selfie." In April of that year, a thirty-two-year-old woman from North Carolina was killed in a head-on collision with a truck. Friends told police she posted a selfie on Facebook while driving and reacting to the popular tune "Happy" by Pharrell Williams.[11]

A nursing student from Poland fell to her death the same year as she was taking a selfie along a bridge while touring Seville, Spain.[12] In Italy a teenager suffered several broken bones and a number of other serious injuries after taking a selfie during a school field trip in the southern part of the country. She fell sixty feet onto the jagged rocks below and eventually died from those injuries.[13] Or how about the twenty-one-year-old man from northern Mexico who wanted to take a selfie so badly that he used his gun as a prop for the photo? That "prop" discharged and shot him in the head.[14] Another "death by selfie" story involved a sixty-year-old woman from Japan who fell down a flight of steps at the Taj Mahal.[15] The government of Russia has gone so far as to issue a *How Not to Take Selfies* pamphlet. The "safe selfie" campaign was launched in the summer of 2015. The campaign and materials were the result of some of the selfie scary stories already mentioned.[16]

Selfies have become so common that the word *selfie* now has its own place in the Oxford dictionary. "A photograph that one has taken of oneself, typically one taken with a smartphone or webcam and shared via social media." Oxford even referred to 2013 as "the year of the selfie." The term *selfie* was also the 2013 word of the year.[17]

According to Google there are some ninety-three million selfies taken each day on Android devices around the world.[18] According to the Pew Research Center, more than half of Millennials (ages eighteen to thirty-three) have taken and shared selfies. According to the same Pew report, those who've grown up with the new digital technologies of the twenty-first century are the heaviest users. By comparison, only six in ten Baby Boomers (those born between 1956 and 1964) and a third of the Silent Generation (those born between 1920s and the 1940s) are caught up in the selfie craze.[19]

The young-adult Millennial group is at least somewhat aware that, according to this Pew survey, owning and using the latest technological toy does have its drawbacks. According to the survey, nine-in-ten Millennials say people generally share too much information about themselves online, a view held by similarly lopsided proportions of all older generations.

The TMI factor will be addressed later on, but that's just one huge pitfall of the selfie syndrome. When it comes to the selfie syndrome, as the list of related tragedies illustrates, common sense isn't so common anymore. As Pope Francis stated, the world of communication can cause us to "lose our bearings."

While Danny Bowman, the young Englishman, had a number of other mental issues, medical experts say no one is immune from the challenges posed by the selfie craze. Selfies have been linked to a variety of conditions connected to a person's obsession with looks, including narcissism and other addictions.

Psychology Today is one of the well-known secular publications that has taken a close look at the recent phenomenon. Media psychologist Dr. Pamela Rutledge blogs for the magazine.

> Selfies frequently trigger perceptions of self-indulgence or attention-seeking social dependence that raises the damned-if-you-do and damned-if-you-don't spectrum of either narcissism or low self-esteem.[20]

Self-indulgence and attention-seeking are not exactly phrases commonly associated with the life of a committed Christian. As we've already seen, they can get us into all kinds of trouble. But just the opposite happens when we practice the virtue of kindness and generosity. Rude, insulting, or even harmful behavior goes out the window, and we're all the better for it.

A Woman in Need of Healing

The hemorrhaging woman in Mark's Gospel is a wonderful example of this. If anyone had reason to be rude and barge forcefully through the crowds to get to Jesus, she did.

> Now there was a woman who had been suffering from hemorrhages for twelve years. She had endured much under many physicians, and had spent all that she had; and she was no better, but rather grew worse. She had heard about Jesus, and came up behind him in the crowd and touched his cloak, for she said, "If I but touch his clothes, I will be made well." Immediately her hemorrhage stopped; and she felt in her body that she was healed of her disease. Immediately aware that power had gone forth from him, Jesus turned about in the crowd and said, "Who touched my clothes?" And his disciples said to him, "You see the crowd pressing in on you; how can you say, 'Who touched me?'" He looked all around to see who had done it. But the woman, knowing what had happened to her, came in fear and trembling, fell down before him, and told him the whole truth. He said to her, "Daughter, your faith has made you well; go in peace, and be healed of your disease." (Mark 5:25–34)

This is a beautiful chapter to meditate upon when it comes to saying good-bye to selfish behavior. Although St. Mark doesn't tell us why this woman didn't draw major attention to herself, screaming out for the Lord to heal her on the spot, you get the sense that she recognized she wasn't the only one in need. St. Mark describes the scene that day as one with wall-to-wall people; so much so that the apostles got annoyed with Jesus when he asked them who touched his cloak. The crowds were obviously smothering them so much so that trying to find out who touched his robe seemed utterly ridiculous.

This woman, however, knew it wasn't all about her. She wasn't the center of the universe. Could it be that, because of her own amount of suffering, she was keenly aware that someone else might need the Lord's help just as much if not more? Unlike some of the other subjects in the countless selfie stories that make the news, the hemorrhaging woman was generous. Reading between the lines, she chose not to dominate Jesus's time or attention. She was so humble that when Jesus started asking questions, she dropped to her knees in gratitude. How much better our world would be if we learned to be more like the woman healed in Mark's Gospel.

We're called to seek first God's kingdom. Jesus, once again, continually reminds us that if we want to save our life we must lay it down and put others first. As followers of Christ, we believe we are in the world but not of the world; we like to think that we have our priorities in order. However, given that we're under so much constant cultural pressure to do just the opposite of what our faith requires, there's no time like the present to gain a deeper self-awareness about what really matters in life.

Come to the Quiet

I've always found it comforting that my favorite saint, who was quite the talker and a true extrovert, is known around the world as one of the greatest mystics. St. Teresa of Avila's social skills were, as she explains so often in her writings, both a gift and a curse. This doctor of the Church, who gave us such classics on the spiritual life as her famous *Interior Castle*, had a jovial and outgoing personality. These traits enabled her to connect with princes, clergy, and laity in her stunning efforts to reform the Carmelite order.

In her early years as a religious, however, her "gift of gab" and her love of socializing caused her to become weak in her prayer life and her overall relationship with God. Gradually she realized that she needed to learn how to use her gifts more wisely, which meant making more time for meditation and less time meeting and greeting friends who frequented the convent seeking her company as well as her spiritual advice. As she grew in her faith, St. Teresa became the first to admit that the call to quiet is no easy task. And maybe that's why the idea of pondering or quieting ourselves has become in many ways such a foreign or odd concept.

We live in a post-Christian society where even among people of faith bumper stickers such as "God is my copilot" have become popular. We're driving this bus, thank you, and God, the Alpha and the Omega and King of Kings, is just along for the ride in case we hit some bumps in the road and have a flat tire. A sincere *call to quiet* can be a little disquieting (no pun intended) and extremely challenging. It should make us realize that God is God—and we are not—and he is also in the driver's seat.

> As I see it, we shall never succeed in knowing ourselves unless we seek to know God. Let us think of His

> greatness and then come back to our own baseness. By looking at His purity we will see our foulness. By meditating on His humility we shall see how far we are from being humble.[21]

St. Teresa, who lived in the fifteenth century, obviously didn't have cell phones, the Internet, or several hundred satellite radio and TV stations vying for her attention and disturbing her peace. But her "Chatty Cathy" approach to life was leading to more socializing and less prayerful solitude. When she faced into this, St. Teresa did not head for the hills and remove herself completely from human interaction. Gradually, however, she became determined to spend more time with God and a little less time in the convent parlor with the local duchess and duke. She learned to understand her weaknesses and temptations while never losing her zest for life and her jovial personality.

Fast-forward five hundred years. In the twenty-first century, thanks to Facebook, Skype, FaceTime, and dozens of other virtual connections, the amount of socializing available to us has multiplied to levels that St. Teresa couldn't have ever imagined. Now is a good time, with St. Teresa in mind, to think about ways we can scale back some of that socializing by removing ourselves from the virtual parlor.

It may sound daunting, but it is possible. Why not start by turning your cell phone off once you get home at night or when the rest of the family returns from school and work? As you reconnect with your loved ones face-to-face, remember to do the same with the Lord before you go to bed. It can be as simple as just taking time to reflect upon the day and saying a brief prayer of thanksgiving before your head hits the pillow. Reflect upon how you feel when you're somewhat detached from technology. Your conversations with family and with God, especially at first, won't necessarily be like a scene from *Little House on the Prairie* or a rerun of *The Waltons*. But they don't have to be. What counts is the effort to bring that call to quiet into your life daily. As St. Teresa reminds us, "The smallest thing when done for the love of God is priceless."[22]

Time for Self-Reflection

- Be honest with yourself and the Lord and consider this question:
- What concerns you most about being challenged to spend less time with your cell phone and more time with God and family?

—CHAPTER THREE—

The Kim Kardashian Craze

The Elusive Search for Attention, Affirmation, and Fame

In the future everyone will be famous for fifteen minutes.

—ANDY WARHOL

Artist Andy Warhol reportedly made that statement way back in 1968, at an exhibition of his work at the Moderna Museet in Stockholm, Sweden. That was nearly five decades ago, long before anyone had ever heard of the Internet or cell phones and selfies. He did hit a nerve in terms of our desire for attention, affirmation, and fame. Thanks to the explosion of modern media technology, the fame factor lasts a lot longer than fifteen minutes, and it has a far more lasting impact than Warhol ever could have imagined.

There is perhaps no better contemporary example of this than Kim Kardashian, a multimillionaire entrepreneur known around the world as the "selfie queen." She is a household name, with a long list of products to go along with it. Though she is considered a fashion icon, she has no distinctive talent, except possibly her business savvy. As she said in a 2009 *Cosmopolitan* interview, "I am an entrepreneur. Ambitious is my middle name."[23]

Her relationships and often-shameful escapades are covered nonstop by the press. Her company even created a fashion mobile game for teens and tweens, with other games following. The games play into the selfie syndrome ten times over. In order to score points or win at "Kim Kardashian Hollywood," for example, players need to move up the celebrity ladder by gaining more fans. They also score points or more celebrity status by having the best clothes and cars and getting as many modeling and acting gigs as possible. The goal is to move one's celebrity status from the E List to the D List and beyond.

Not exactly wholesome messages for girls and women are they? Nevertheless, her games continue to break Internet sales records. Originally released in June of 2014, the first game earned $1.6 million in just five days. Kardashian strikes a note with those wanting those fifteen minutes of fame and more. It gives players a chance to keep up with the Joneses, the Kardashians, and everybody else for that matter, by living out their own version of Hollywood stardom.

Kardashian is basically sitting at the helm of an empire that all began with her fifteen minutes of fame on a silly, egocentric reality TV show featuring the exploits of her family (including her stepfather, Bruce, now Caitlyn, Jenner). *Keeping Up with the Kardashians* skyrocketed to popularity through the help of one selfie after another uploaded on Facebook and retweeted around the world. At last count Kardashian had close to thirty-seven million followers on Twitter alone, plus millions of followers on Facebook and Instagram.

In spring 2015 Kim Kardashian published a book, appropriately entitled *Selfish,* which quickly became a best seller. The hardcover is nothing more than *hundreds* of pages of selfies, some of them risqué, others she risked her life taking. Apparently Kardashian started taking selfies way back in 1984, so the book is arranged chronologically over the past thirty years.

In 2015 Kim Kardashian was named one of *Time* magazine's thirty most influential people on the Internet. According to *Time*:

> She may tout millions of fans in real life, but Kardashian truly stands out on Instagram. There, she has perfected the art of the selfie: some with famous friends, some in luxurious bathrooms, and all to the delight of her [millions] of followers. Long a performer in a reality TV show produced and edited by others, Kardashian also deftly uses Twitter to define and defend her own narrative ("Her eyes were closed and I was feeling my look! Can I live?!?" she sniped after being criticized for cropping her daughter out of a selfie), and of course to promote her various business ventures.[24]

Anyone with even an ounce of concern about the culture and how Christians and others are influenced by it should pay attention to the rise of Kim Kardashian and the success of her book. *The Bookseller's* features editor Tom Tivnan told *The Guardian* newspaper in England that Kardashian has caught the public's eye in a major way.

> Seriously, one of the reasons its doing so well is Kim Kardashian is our dirty little secret. Even those who rail against her in the "why is she famous, she has no talent" vein often pop over to the "sidebar of shame" to find out what she and Kanye are up to.[25]

Kardashian's popularity and stardom have baffled and bothered many experts, including sociology professor and author Pepper Schwartz.

> Why are young women entranced with this woman? (I understand why young men would be.) But young girls who are easily impressionable and hooked by hype may be enchanted with the ease with which she seems to float through life and take on her "struggles" (Which brand name shall I buy? Which mini-feud will I rage about?) as ones they would rather have than the ones they have in real life.
>
> They envy her. The fact is that the Kardashians have gained traction in their lives. They have built an empire and no one can deny she and her posse have figured out how to make a fortune based on her brand. Kim K won't be around forever. But is it some failure of feminism among the young that allows this kind of person to be a star?[26]

Schwartz wrote the stinging op-ed on *Selfish* shortly before the book was published, encouraging folks not to buy it. The professor suggested that if the book was a dud, sales wise this would serve as a positive sign that our society hasn't gone completely off the rails.

> So wouldn't it be great if Kim K's selfie book sat moldering in bookstores and on Amazon? That would reassure me about the soul of modern girls and young women. I wouldn't blame anyone for paging through it. It's a little like a car wreck—awful, but hard to totally avoid looking at. But buying the book is another thing altogether.
>
> Instead of sending Kim K to the bank, let's encourage her to go to a really good therapist. This kind of narcissism needs to be treated, not celebrated.[27]

Her hopes were short-lived, to say the least. *Selfish* rose to the top of the best-seller list on both sides of the Atlantic within days of being released.

I often wonder if Kim Kardashian's popularity and huge success say more about society than they do about the reality TV star herself. Only God knows what is truly in a person's heart, but Jesus also tells us in Matthew 7:16 that "you will know them by their fruits." What type of fruit are Kim and the rest of the Kardashian clan bearing? Kardashian and her siblings continue to be the topic of the entertainment talk shows as they move from one troubled relationship to another. Despite their fame and fortune, are they truly happy? And why are the lives of the rich, famous, and frivolous so attractive that people around the globe are practically glued to their every move?

We were made for relationship, and—as shallow as the Kardashian relationships seem to be—our technology can falsely make us feel like we are a part of their world, a world that on the surface seems so much more glamorous and exciting than ours.

Years ago, when I was still working as a broadcast journalist, my job often required me to follow up on crime stories by knocking on doors in a variety of different neighborhoods. More than once I walked into a home during the middle of the day where family members were glued to the TV, talking about the characters in the daytime drama as if they were relatives or close acquaintances rather than actors playing a part. It was as though the situations being portrayed on television were real, and the drama that had touched their own lives was the illusion.

Now in addition to coming into millions of homes through reality TV shows, the Kim Kardashians of the world continue to catch our attention through nonstop social media saturation. But how many of their fans ever stop to think about whether the Kardashians are actually living fulfilling lives? Do most assume that the combination of money and being a household name automatically equals utter bliss? Scripture, not to mention plenty of studies, along with the good old Beatles, tell us money—or more specifically, the love of it—can't buy us love or true contentment. But that doesn't seem to stop millions from tuning in for another fix of the famous and financially fortunate.

Because of their prevalence in our lives, they prey on our deepest desires. It's not wrong to want nice things or desire to be successful, but it is wrong to think that those things can provide deep and long-term satisfaction. Keeping up with the Kardashians keeps us tied down to the world.

If you think Catholics on the periphery, those who have fallen away from their faith, are the only Christians following the shenanigans of the Kim Kardashian types, think again. Far too often I hear some pretty frustrating and quite sad statements from Catholics in the pews and those who listen to my daily radio show. Maybe they haven't taken the plunge and spent twenty dollars of their hard-earned money on ridiculous books such as *Selfish*. But they certainly are overly influenced by what they see in the culture. Christian women especially are constantly comparing themselves to images on the Internet, in magazines, and on TV, including reality TV.

In addition, I hear from moms who regularly struggle with their tween and teen daughters over appropriate clothing. Where do we think tweens and teens are getting their fashion cues? As Schwartz mentioned, Kardashian has "gained traction with" them.

The carefree lifestyle of moving from one party or one relationship to the next is also gaining traction. Wouldn't it be nice if all we had to worry about was which outfit we were going to wear to the next Hollywood bash? If problems crop up in a relationship, no worries; move on to the next guy. Anything goes as long as the need for happiness is being met.

We see an awful lot of what appears to be glitz and glamour, fun and games, out there in the virtual world. What we don't see is a decent dose of "real life"—a glimpse of people actually working through problems and making sacrifices. Thanks to the Kardashians of the world, couples with difficulties think their issues can and should be solved in a matter of days or weeks.

On average young people consume between fifty-four to sixty hours of media per week. Adults consume about forty to forty-five hours per week. Now, I would like to think that the Catholics represented in those statistics are spending those hours listening to Catholic radio and watching Catholic television, but that's simply not the case. My voice on the radio is just one of many. My voice is often drowned out by an onslaught of messages that run counter to what we believe. How do I know that? Well, when it comes to what the pope says or what the Church teaches, more often than not faithful Catholics ask me, "Why did the pope say this, that, or the other thing?" or "Why is the Church teaching this?" when they should be asking *if* instead of *why*.

Our self-centered world can easily lead us to believe that life should be all about us—it's all about whatever makes us happy.

We are free to do whatever we want with whomever because we are the center of our own universe. And even if we don't become famous for fifteen minutes, time in the spotlight will certainly help us, or so we like to think, on our path to fulfillment.

Quiz Time: Do You Use Media—Or Does Media Use You?

Take this short quiz to uncover the truth about your family's media consumption.

1. How long has it been since you spent an entire weekend without turning on the television?
   a. Last weekend.
   b. Last month—we took our family camping.
   c. I think it was that blizzard about eight years ago. It got pretty ugly until we found batteries for the Gameboy.
2. The electricity just went out! What's the most likely first response?
   a. All right! Build a fire, make some s'mores, and let's have a game night!
   b. Uh, oh. Where's my emergency stash of batteries?
   c. OK, where can we crash tonight so the kids don't drive us crazy?
3. If you could switch places with anyone in the world for a day, who would it be?
   a. One of the characters on your favorite BBC drama.
   b. Kim Kardashian.
   c. That mother in your homeschool group, so you can get her secret recipe for double-chocolate granola squares.

The studies on selfies continue to pile up. Researchers say selfies and other material viewed online can be influential for children when it comes to their sense of self. The same researchers say adults also make strong connections to what they see on the Internet. While that might be true, in the end—surprise, surprise—none of this makes us happy. In fact, it can make us feel worse about ourselves because we are comparing our lives to others'.

In 2013, for example, researchers at the University of Michigan studied eighty-two young adults and their Facebook accounts for two weeks. The more time the study participants spent on Facebook, the more dissatisfied they were with their lives.[28] Another study out of Germany had similar results, according to Hanna Krasnova from the Institute of Information Systems at Berlin's Humboldt University:

> We were surprised by how many people have a negative experience from Facebook with envy leaving them feeling lonely, frustrated or angry. The spread and ubiquitous presence of envy on Social Networking Sites is shown to undermine users' life satisfaction.[29]

The study's results showed something else Krasnova found interesting. The negative feeling of envy led to the participants boasting more on social media about their achievements in an attempt to show themselves in a more positive light. Men posted more self-promotional content in an effort to let people know about all their accomplishments. Women stressed appearance and social lives.

The search for fame and affirmation in our selfie-driven society is proving to be a vicious cycle. The efforts to seek attention and the need to be loved are not new to us. But what *is* new are the ways people are pursuing attention, affirmation, and fame in hopes of making their dreams quickly come true. The more we keep promoting ourselves in hopes of at least getting noticed, the more closed in on ourselves we become, and the more miserable we become because we just can't seem to measure up.

Keeping Up with the Kardashians—or Simply Being Content

What is the antidote for measuring ourselves by such false standards? Simplicity. Contentment. No matter how much material wealth we might have, we can choose to live simply. We can learn to be content with what we have, free of the insatiable desire to continually amass more. Instead of chasing after fame, we can focus on doing and being our best.

Queen Esther is a good example of someone, who despite her beauty and good fortune, had her priorities in order. Her life was anchored in God and she was content to place her life in his hands, even though by doing so, she was taking a risk.

In the Old Testament we learn how the king adored Queen Esther, a Jew. She dressed in the finest clothes and jewels and lived a life of sheer luxury. However, even a queen had to be summoned before meeting with the king. Approaching the king without an invitation was an act punishable by death. But none of that mattered to Queen Esther; nothing was more important to her than her God and her people, who were being threatened.

Before she went to the king to ask him to spare the lives of her people, she humbled herself in prayer and put herself totally in God's hands. "I will go to the king," she said, "though it is against the law; [and here is my favorite verse from the story of Esther] and if I perish, I perish" (Esther 13:16).

If only we could have that kind of faith and contentment in God's will.

There are twenty-first–century role models who have provided wonderful examples of how to live a virtuous life, but unfortunately they don't garner nearly as much press as reality TV stars. A case in point is college basketball star Lauren Hill, who passed away from a malignant brain tumor in April 2015. She was determined, however, to continue playing basketball during her treatment. Lauren also thought it was important to use her remaining time on earth helping other cancer patients, so she started an organization to raise money and awareness for cancer research. By the time she died, over $1.5 million had been donated to her The Cure Starts Now Foundation. Lauren's courage led to her being nominated posthumously for the prestigious Arthur Ashe Courage Award given by ESPN at the ESPYs. Ironically or maybe not so ironically, given what the world covets, the award went instead to transgender Bruce Jenner. Jenner was also chosen over Iraq war veteran star Noah Galloway who lost most of an arm and one of his legs fighting for his country.

These types of stories can serve as aha moments or wake-up calls in your life, helping you to discern media messages and media usage. What do they say about what the world values versus what God wants us to value?

It's one thing to use technology for good—maybe we're sharing helpful information or raising awareness for a charitable cause. Maybe we're keeping in closer contact with friends and family and making new friends as well. The Church affirms, over and over again, this type of media application in our lives. Pope Francis is not alone in his attempts to guide us in using the Internet to promote what's true, beautiful, and good. His predecessor, Pope Benedict XVI, did the same:

> These spaces, when engaged in a wise and balanced way, help to foster forms of dialogue and debate which, if conducted respectfully and with concern for privacy, responsibility and truthfulness, can reinforce the bonds of unity between individuals and effectively promote the harmony of the human family. The exchange of information can become true communication, links ripen into friendships, and connections facilitate communion. If the networks are called to realize this great potential, the people involved in them must make an effort to be authentic since, in these spaces, it is not only ideas and information that are shared, but ultimately our very selves.
>
> The development of social networks calls for commitment: people are engaged in building relationships and making friends, in looking for answers to their questions and being entertained, but also in finding intellectual stimulation and sharing knowledge and know-how. The networks are increasingly becoming part of the very fabric of society, inasmuch as they bring people together on the basis of these fundamental needs. *Social networks are thus nourished by aspirations rooted in the human heart.*[30]

That last line of the above quote is key. What aspirations do we see when we look around on the Internet and elsewhere? Too many of us, due to media influence combined with unpleasant challenges or personal disappointments, are allowing the wrong aspirations to shape our lives.

Come to the Quiet

There is a beautiful prayer attributed to Fr. Pedro Arrupe, S.J., entitled "Fall in Love" that my husband and I use when we lead retreats. While we find it particularly moving when speaking before married couples, the words of this powerful prayer speak to all of us about the need to more closely examine what our day-to-day activities say about our priorities.

> Nothing is more practical than finding God,
> than falling in Love in a quite absolute, final way.
> What you are in love with,
> what seizes your imagination, will affect everything.
> It will decide what will get you out of bed in the morning,
> what you do with your evenings,
> how you spend your weekends,
> what you read, whom you know,
> what breaks your heart,
> and what amazes you with joy and gratitude.
> Fall in Love, stay in love,
> and it will decide everything. [31]

Secular research actually backs up what our faith continues to teach us: It's not all about us. And what we're all really seeking, even if we don't know it, as Pope St. John Paul II reminded young people at the first World Youth Day in Denver, the ultimate source of love, affirmation, and fulfillment is Jesus:

> It is Jesus that you seek when you dream of happiness; He is waiting for you when nothing else you find satisfies you; He is the beauty to which you are so attracted; it is He who provoked you with that thirst for fullness that will not let you settle for compromise; it is He who urges you to shed the masks of a false life; it is He

who reads in your heart your most genuine choices, the choices that others try to stifle.[32]

Time for Self-Reflection

Now would be a good time to reflect on who or what you are seeking. Is it Jesus? Is it the longing for a deeper relationship with him that gets you out of bed each morning, occupies your time in the evenings, and seizes your imagination? If not, how might your media habits be impacting your relationship with God?

—CHAPTER FOUR—

Me, My Selfie, and I or Father, Son, and Holy Spirit

The Unhealthy Trio vs. The Holy Trinity

> Selfishness must be discovered and understood before it can be removed. It is powerless to remove itself, neither will it pass away of itself.
>
> Darkness ceases only when light is introduced; so ignorance can only be dispersed by knowledge and selfishness by love.[33]
>
> —JAMES ALLEN

In 2015 the film *War Room* was a surprising success. Not too many critics expected the film to be even a blip on the box-office radar screen when it opened on Labor Day weekend. However, it proved to be an even bigger hit than the earlier films produced by the same men who gave us *Fireproof* and *Courageous,* two other low-budget Christian films that held their own earnings-wise.

War Room tells the story of a young married couple, the Jordans. They appear to have it all: great jobs, a beautiful home, and a wonderful daughter. But as the old saying goes, looks can be deceiving. We soon learn that Tony and Elizabeth's seemingly idyllic marriage is in reality a war zone. Tony is a workaholic, spending more and more hours away from his wife and daughter as he rakes in the big bucks from his pharmaceutical sales job. He also begins to flirt with a coworker. Elizabeth is becoming increasingly bitter, angry, and suspicious. When they are home together, they fight constantly.

You'll have to rent it if you want to know how it ends and whether the many issues are resolved. But it is a powerful illustration on the big screen of how a selfish approach to life impacts the world around us, even if we don't realize it. We see Tony and Elizabeth's daughter torn apart by neglect and loneliness, not to mention the stress of worrying about her parents possibly divorcing. Tony's hunger for more money leads him to steal from his company. And most of Elizabeth's energy is spent nagging and complaining, which only escalates the cycle of selfish misery. Tony and Elizabeth focus solely on their own individual needs, their hurts, their unmet expectations in the marriage. They fail to look at life and their struggles from each other's perspective.

Sound familiar? Well, apparently the difficult scenes that played out in the movie resonated with a lot of folks. *War Room* hit a big nerve, and as a result a low-budget film hit it big in the box office, becoming the company's highest profile movie to date, and earning over $67 million in less than four months. Not bad for a film that took only about $3 million to make.

OK, so what does *War Room's* positive reception have to do with the selfie craze? Apparently a lot of us have experienced the fallout of selfishness. And that selfishness often is exacerbated when we engage in actions (such as taking selfies) that reinforce a narcissistic world view.

This is what Ohio State Associate Professor of Communications Jesse Fox found when he studied the social media habits of eight hundred men, ages eighteen to forty. The participants completed an online survey asking about their photo-posting behavior on social media. They were also asked if and how they edited those photos. While it is not so surprising that Fox found a correlation between the number of images they posted—and edited—with higher levels of self-objectification and narcissism, he also found a correlation between this behavior and an even more disturbing trait:

> They also score higher on this other anti-social personality trait, psychopathy.... It's not surprising that men who post a lot of selfies and spend more time editing them are more narcissistic, but this is the first time it has actually been confirmed in a study.[34]

The study also found that those who received more feedback from friends tended to have a higher incidence of editing and posting, reinforcing the negative emotional behaviors.

Of course, not every person who likes to take and share selfies is destined to turn into a narcissist or a psychopath. That said, there is a growing amount of research to show why we need to be concerned about the connection between selfies and selfishness. Our interest in selfies says a great deal about our personalities, and not in a positive way. Sometimes, just like Elizabeth and Tony Jordan from *War Room,* we forget that our actions can also have a negative or positive ripple effect that impacts others.

Think about it. If we're spending a lot of time taking, editing, and posting selfies, isn't it pretty obvious who is the center of our universe? It's not God. It's not even family. It's me, myself, and I. Given the size of the actual universe, the view from your cell phone or latest post might make you feel popular, attractive, and sexy, but it also leads nowhere, unless you consider Facebook or Instagram a worthwhile destination.

Me, myself, and I is the exact opposite of who God is in the Holy Trinity. The Trinity, as the Catholic Church has taught for centuries, gives us a true understanding of who we are as human beings. We were meant for relationship, not individualism. God came to us as a family, and we are all part of that family, meant to emulate the same life-giving and selfless exchange. One article on *Catholic Online* describes the Trinity this way:

> This relationship, a bond of life-giving love, is of such depth and magnitude as to be indescribable. It is our Triune God whose life-giving power and love sustains us from moment to moment. It is the Holy Trinity who allows us each breath, provides us with the energy of life, and graces us with that seed of faith deep within our hearts. Yet Christ's revelation of the inner life of God illumines not only our dependence on God, but who we are as persons, how we should relate to others, and how society should function and exist in relation to God. Therefore, the Most Holy Trinity is the Light that enlightens every aspect of the human person.[35]

Once we understand and embrace God as revealed in the Trinity, we can see that this inseparable relationship reveals something profound about who we are because we are made in God's image and likeness. The *Catechism of the Catholic Church* explains that the mystery of the Holy Spirit is "the central mystery of the Christian faith and Christian life" (CCC 267). God reveals himself to us in a relationship—a relationship of Father, Son, and Holy Spirit.

Noted philosopher, author, and speaker Fr. Robert Spitzer agrees that one of the problems of our selfie-minded culture is the inability to reach beyond ourselves, to reflect, contemplate, and wonder about all but the most basic questions that tug or should tug at the human heart. Who am I? Why am I here? Where am I going? He calls this the loss of transcendence. Such a loss then leads to a host of other problems, problems with far-reaching effects. He sees this as causing four key consequences connected to a serious lack of being able to see beyond our own noses:

- An underestimation of our nature, dignity, destiny, and meaning in life;
- An absence of an important source of healing and consolation for those who are suffering and sick;
- Alienation from reality, others, and ourselves, negatively impacting suicide rates, family relations, substance abuse, and sense of fulfillment and hope;
- A decline in ethical motivation within individuals and ethical conduct within culture.[36]

Maybe you think Fr. Spitzer is stretching it a bit. Seriously, are a few selfies among friends really all that big of a deal? No, of course not, but we're not talking about just a few selfies. We're talking about an attitude helped along by the selfie culture that is now permeating society.

Falling Out of Eden: Losing Our Transcendence

In lieu of a quiz this time, let's go through Fr. Spitzer's four points one by one. Do you recognize yourself in any of these symptoms?

1. **An underestimation and desperation of our nature, dignity, destiny, and meaning in life.** When we consider the Holy Trinity

and the fact that we were designed in the image and likeness of God, we realize that we are actually going against our nature and dignity when become self-involved.

Think about the Ohio State University study that illustrated the connection between frequent selfies and an increase in narcissistic behavior. How can a self-absorbed person relate or even begin to comprehend giving of themselves in a familial relationship such as marriage or parenthood? Do Elizabeth and Tony Jordan of *War Room* come to mind perhaps? The Jordans had lost sight of all of the beautiful things Fr. Spitzer mentions. They had forgotten their true nature and dignity.

Pope St. John Paul II said that we don't find ourselves until we lose ourselves in Christ. In other words, true happiness only comes from commitment and self-sacrifice. Throughout the Bible, in particular the New Testament, we see what is a contradiction by the world's standard spelled out over and over again. When we lose our life for love's sake, we gain it back tenfold. That's the heart of the Christian message, and it's the only way we will reach our true destination: heaven.

- "Those who love their life lose it, and those who hate their life in this world will keep it for eternal life." (John 12:25)
- "We know love by this, that he laid down his life for us—and we ought to lay down our lives for one another." (1 John 3:16)
- "If you wish to be perfect, go, sell your possessions, and give the money to the poor, and you will have treasure in heaven; then come, follow me." (Matthew 19:21)

2. An absence of an important source of healing and consolation for those who are suffering and sick. Unless you live underground or in a cave somewhere, you're most likely all too familiar with the incredibly popular Disney film *Frozen*. You can probably recite the lyrics to the hit tune "Let It Go" forward and backward and then some. When I first heard that song on the radio, I was really troubled by the "me, myself, and I" message of the song; I thought it was setting a horrible example for young people. To make matters worse, the song was everywhere, and the movie practically spawned a separate industry through the soundtrack and endless array of toys, clothing, and other items related to it. There were constant reminders for Elsa fans everywhere to "let it go" (and to heck with everybody else). When I finally saw the film, however, I realized that both the song and the film offer some very teachable moments for adults and children alike as Queen Elsa belts out "Let It Go" from a mountaintop in the middle of the woods.

At first it seems that the song's lyrics might be saying there's no right or wrong, no rules, no absolutes. Yikes. That's not good. But when you look at the song in context, you realize Elsa was actually trapped in an ice castle—the isolated world she had built for herself. Her feelings and ego had taken quite a few hits because her own subjects no longer trusted her after her ice powers left the kingdom of Arendelle in an eternal winter. Can you blame them? Well, she did. So she stormed off, quite literally, and left everything and everyone behind, including her sister, Princess Anna, and her responsibilities as queen. She was oblivious to the damage she had done, even though some of it was unintentional.

There was, as Fr. Spitzer said, "an absence" of that important source of healing and consolation. She was numb (frozen) to those who were sick and suffering. She allowed her hurt to control her. The hurt turned to anger, and as that anger grew stronger, so did her ice powers. But even with all of that power, Elsa was not happy while holed up in the ice castle. She was miserable and self-centered, thinking only about her own pain.

It's a good lesson as to how much damage we can do and how unhappy we can become when we are concentrating for the most part on ourselves and thinking only about what we are feeling or experiencing in the current moment. In the end it was the self-sacrifice of Princess Anna that melts Elsa's hardened heart, along with everything else that had frozen in Arendelle as well.

3. Alienation from reality, others, and ourselves, negatively impacting suicide rates, family relations, substance abuse, and sense of fulfillment and hope. Remember Danny Bowman, the teen from England? His obsession with grabbing the perfect selfie led to addictive behavior, an attempted suicide, and hospitalization. He perfectly illustrates this point, with alienation from reality being at the top of the list.

What type of media messages are we consuming? How does so much media consumption alter our view of reality? How are we being desensitized by the messages? How much time does posting selfies, surfing the Internet, or playing computer games take away from our family and other priorities? Do we realize how all of this might be affecting our sense of fulfillment? Our sense of hope?

4. A decline in ethical motivation within individuals and ethical conduct within culture. Where do we begin with this point? Let's start with a very unscientific survey. If you believe that ethics and morality in general have taken a nosedive in recent years, raise your hand. I actually ask that question at my seminars and media awareness presentations, and every time I get the same response: Just about every hand in the room goes up quickly and firmly.

But even though most of us agree with this answer, too many of us aren't all that motivated to do anything about it. We're too wrapped up in our own worlds, simply trying to get through the day. Even among those who find the Kim Kardashian clan utterly ridiculous, there are plenty who still grab the remote because they can't resist not seeing the latest and greatest. Not to pile on Kim Kardashian, but in so many ways she is the poster child for what can go wrong when we take ourselves too seriously. At the end of the day, what type of contribution does she inspire her followers to make to the culture and to the world?

Our lack of transcendence, according to Fr. Spitzer, has been with us since the early twentieth century, undermining our belief system, so much so that many people today find it difficult to believe in God and the human soul.

> The materialist perspective has not only cast its spell on the natural sciences, psychology, philosophy and literature, it also has enthralled popular culture, which offers very little to encourage the "soul's upward yearning."
>
> ...It's almost as if we have regressed to a pre-Platonic state in which many really don't care whether they are living for the fullest possible purpose, dignity, and destiny. It's as if some huge cultural propaganda machine has talked us out of believing that such an ideal is possible-and we really believe it and submit to a

> life that is second third, or fourth rate by Platonic standards, settling for entertainment rather than enlightenment, for "good" times instead of contribution, for being admired instead of loving and being loved, and for image instead of reality.[37]

Living for the Moment vs. Living Life on Purpose

In its 2014 Religious Landscape Study, the Pew Research Center on Religious and Public Life indirectly confirmed Fr. Robert Spitzer's keen observations. According to Pew, fewer and fewer people are looking upward. As a matter of fact, there was another drop in the overall rate of religious belief and practice among Americans. While Pew also found some stability among people who belong to an organized religion, the number of those identifying as "nones," those no longer having any religious affiliation, continues to grow.

> The falloff in traditional religious beliefs and practices coincides with changes in the religious composition of the U.S. public. A growing share of Americans are religiously unaffiliated, including some who self-identify as atheists or agnostics as well as many who describe their religion as "nothing in particular." Altogether, the religiously unaffiliated (also called the "nones") now account for 23% of the adult population, up from 16% in 2007.[38]

This lack of transcendence is all too common today. The group described as the "nones" is merely hanging out in the here and now. It's a very empty and sad way to live, according to the dynamic Italian college student who would become the patron saint for World Youth Day, Blessed Pierre Giorgio Frassati. He said: "To live without a patrimony to defend, without a steady struggle for truth, that is not living but existing."[39]

Hanging out in the here and now, or living for the moment, is not to be confused with living that moment fully, however. To live fully in the present requires having an understanding of the big picture—a transcendent view, an eternal perspective. That infuses each and every moment with meaning and purpose, peace and joy. Instead of merely enjoying one empty pleasure after another, each day is full of new opportunities to grow and give.

Come to the Quiet

We were made for a lot more than just existing. Jesus tells us that He wants all of us to be filled with joy, not only now, but forever. "I came that they may have life, and have it abundantly" (John 10:10).

St. Paul tells us that most of us have no idea how much God has in store for us. "What no eye has seen, nor ear heard, nor the human heart conceived, what God has prepared for those who love him—these things God has revealed to us through the Spirit" (1 Corinthians 2:9–10).

We all long for happiness, but we might be settling for merely existing because we have grown comfortable thinking that total autonomy and satisfying our immediate needs and desires are all we can hope for. Scripture and the teachings of the Church tell us that there is so much more for us to do here on earth and eventually in heaven. Take some time to examine what the *Catechism* says about heaven:

> This perfect life with the Most Holy Trinity—this communion of life and love with the Trinity, with the Virgin Mary, the angels and all the blessed—is called "heaven." Heaven is the ultimate end and fulfillment of the deepest human longings, the state of supreme, definitive happiness. (CCC 1024).

See how many Scripture verses you can find about finding true and lasting joy. Spend some time reflecting on how your life compares with what God promises. Get out your journal and write about how your actions and view of the world may be preventing you from having that abundant life.

Time for Self-Reflection

- When was the last time, if ever, you pondered what it means to be made in the image and likeness of God?
- Are you living your life as an example of that familial godly image?

—CHAPTER FIVE—

To Thine "Real" Self Be True

Rediscovering Our True Identity as Children of God

> If I ever go looking for my heart's desire again,
> I won't look any further than my own back yard.
> Because if it isn't there, I never really lost it to
> begin with.[40]
>
> —L. Frank Baum

Dorothy discovered the truth the hard way. She ran away from her Kansas farm looking for someplace safer where she and her precious little dog Toto could live trouble-free and happily ever after, only to discover that home really is where the heart is. Before she took off for greener pastures, she was absolutely convinced that there was something bigger and better out there for her. She couldn't stop thinking, dreaming, and singing about it. She spent a lot of time imagining herself far from the fields of Kansas.

Although Dorothy lived a very simple life in the Sunflower State, a life so drastically different from our high-tech world of the twenty-first century, the reason her story remains so popular is because it is a timeless and a relatable one. We all are looking for our "heart's desire," and we often search for it in all the wrong places, including the Internet and social media sites.

Veteran journalist and author Sue Ellen Browder is concerned about all the Dorothys out there whose journey for happiness is guided by false expectations built up by an extremely dominant culture. Browder's articles have appeared in a long list of popular magazines, including *Cosmopolitan, Woman's Day,* and *Reader's Digest,* and she has been immersed in the influential media world for decades. She says:

> The most insidious results of my over-focus on the "media culture" around me were internal. All the media noise kept me focused outward on symbols of "success" (money, power, fame, etc.) while my interior relationship to God languished. On the outside, I was becoming more and more successful. Yet I was frequently anxious or depressed, but didn't know why. This interior turmoil led to all sorts of false choices, because when my mind and body were flooded with stress hormones, I couldn't think clearly. Without a close relationship to the Father, the Son and the Holy Spirit and, therefore, without truth, goodness, beauty and love to guide me, I was constantly making bad choices. I even had an abortion.[41]

Browder has chronicled her journey as a writer, feminist, and eventual Catholic convert in her eye-opening book *Subverted: How I Helped the Sexual Revolution Hijack the Women's Movement.* She was trained at the prestigious University of Missouri School of Journalism as an investigative reporter, but due to her desire for success, she quickly betrayed that training, becoming a propagandist for the sexual revolution along with her colleagues at *Cosmopolitan* and other publications. She and her coworkers regularly invented—yes, invented—sources and scenarios in order to get people to buy into the free-for-all life style of the "Cosmo Girl" who was supposedly jumping from bed to bed and having a grand old time enjoying life on the town. The sexual revolution was portrayed in articles designed to soft-sell sex outside of marriage, contraception, and abortion, along with promoting the corner office as every woman's road to that place somewhere over the rainbow.

Sue Ellen was heavily influenced by the ideas she was helping to promote, especially the emphasis on women pursuing their goals, choices, and freedom at any cost. And mind you, there wasn't a selfie, cell phone, or laptop in sight, so how much more are we influenced given the insidious nature of the media now? That's why Browder is so concerned about the Dorothys among us today.

> I would have to say today's ever-present media make the media influence a hundred times worse. I see many young women so locked into their laptops and cell phones that they no longer even seem to engage with the real world around them. It's like living in a tiny, self-enclosed bubble, a tiny rectangular prison in which a young woman may believe she's "connecting" with others when she's actually being blocked from finding her true identity.[42]

Quiz Time: How Does the Media Shape Your Self-Image?

Do you ever stop to consider how the media you watch and read affects the way you look at yourself? Let's take this quiz and find out!

1. How many hours a day, on average, do you watch television (including religious programming)?

a. It's on whenever I'm at home—I like the noise in the background.
b. We watch as a family every night after dinner for at least an hour.
c. At least once a week I go all day without turning on the TV.

2. While standing in line at the grocery store, your eyes fall on a rack of magazines near the register. What's your first reaction?
a. Hmm… Let's check out what my favorite actress is wearing in *People!*
b. Ooh! That dish on the cover of the cooking magazine looks delicious.
c. Yikes. That actress is the same age as me. She looks great—I wonder if she had any work done? (Maybe I should, too?)

3. What's the last thing you see before you go to sleep at night?
a. My favorite crime drama or sitcom.
b. My prayer book or Bible.
c. QVC. I always have a little time to shop!

4. Name a "successful" woman you don't know well but greatly admire. Is she…
a. A political figure.
b. A celebrity or artist.
c. A Catholic writer, blogger, or saint.

There really isn't any right or wrong answer on this quiz (though I don't recommend unnecessary cosmetic surgery!). This is just an opportunity to think about the effects of the media on our priorities and our outlook in both big and little ways. I know I've found that to be true in my own life, especially as I pursued my own career goals.

Sue Ellen and I have a lot in common. We were both trained at prominent journalism schools. We both thought we were living the thoroughly modern American woman's dream. I worked in the secular media for nearly twenty years as a radio and TV news reporter, ignoring just about everything and everyone else in my life, including my husband, in order to get ahead. I started in the news business about ten years after Sue Ellen, and back then I would have considered her a trailblazer for the feminist cause and for truly *liberated* women everywhere. Like her, I was very much influenced by the culture in which I worked. I was raised Catholic, but within my first year of journalism school at Central Michigan University, I stopped going to Mass.

Along the way I ignored the emptiness I was feeling. No matter how much success I achieved, no matter how hard I worked, it was never enough. I was only as good as my last story. In the meantime, I was also impacted by the fallout of the "sex and the single girl" craze that began with Sue Ellen's "anything goes" generation. I had become my own version of a propagandist perpetuating many of the myths of the sexual revolution; myths most of the world had come to accept as fact. Yet at the same time I still referred to myself as a Christian.

So what are girls like Sue Ellen and me doing in a place like the Catholic Church? Both of us experienced a gradual awakening, or transcendence. (There's that fancy word again.) My first "come to Jesus" moment occurred when my local TV station decided not to renew my contract. There I was, unexpectedly walking out the door with a box of belongings in my hand. I was shell-shocked—I no longer had any identity outside the newsroom and the anchor desk. My identity actually had been falsely formed through the messages I was constantly receiving from the culture—the attitude in newsroom, magazine articles, TV shows, movies, and advertising. It was all about grabbing the brass ring and pushing through the glass ceiling, no matter what the cost. Along the way up the ladder, women could and should do whatever they wanted to, not only to get ahead but to be "fulfilled" emotionally, professionally, and of course sexually.

The same culture that convinced me it was "all about me" couldn't have cared less about all the so-called achievements I was encouraged to score in the name of feminism. All I had to show for the many weekends, holidays, and nightshifts I put in was a severance check and a few pencils and pens—oh, and a marriage that was pretty much in shambles.

Thank goodness my husband had come back to the Church about a year before I lost my job. He didn't give up on us; instead he was patient and prayerful. Finally, after six months of unemployment with a lot of time on my hands to think and reflect, I realized I couldn't do it alone anymore. I sent out an unsophisticated S.O.S prayer asking God to come back into my life. Little by little I began to realize what a false existence I had built for myself, one that had come crashing down so quickly.

Sue Ellen's conversion was also gradual, with some aha moments along the way—the first being when she discovered the *Catechism of the Catholic Church*.

> When you're literally languishing and dying in the secular media world, as I was, one place you don't even begin to think to look for a lifeline is in the Catholic Church. The very source of love, truth and happiness—which is Christ Himself—is found in the fullness of the Catholic Church. Yet the media culture in which I lived continually urged me to turn my eyes away from the

> Church and sent me the unspoken message, "Whatever you do, don't look there. That stuffy old Catholic Church doesn't have anything to offer a liberated smart-cookie like you. Don't even bother." … After my husband and I converted to Catholicism, I looked back and realized that Christ had been calling to me all my life. It is always Christ who takes the first step. He is the Truth in Person, and He's the One who calls us. But I was just so caught up in my own ideas and in the media culture around me that I was too deaf and blind to hear Him.[43]

Cultural Conformity vs. Being Conformed to Christ

St. John the Baptist is a good example for us when it comes to opening our eyes and ears to God and gaining a clearer understanding of our true dignity as opposed to what we have invented on our own. In John 3:28 he states loudly and clearly to his followers that he was not "the Christ." He has a clear understanding of his identity and where it comes from. Earlier in this same chapter, he reminds us that everything we have comes from God (see John 3:27); this is another moment of clarity. When we conform to the culture and make up our own rules, we are attempting to play God.

The *Catechism* reminds Christians to recognize their dignity. It encourages us that, unlike Humpty Dumpty, God can put us back together again.

> Remember who is your head and of whose body you are a member. Never forget that you have been rescued from the power of darkness and brought into the light of the Kingdom of God. (CCC 1691)

Fr. Paul Check, the national chaplain for the Courage apostolate, which ministers to Catholic men and women who experience same-sex attraction, explains that we simply don't know who we are any longer. Stop for a moment and think of all of the sexual confusion in our culture right now and all the ways people can "identify" themselves. Facebook offers users some fifty-eight—yes, *fifty-eight*!—different gender options. Fr. Check says the real issue is not sex or even relationships; it comes down to what he refers to as a "poverty" that leads to a misdirected desire for fulfillment.

> The poverty to which I refer is a confusion or lack of some level of understanding about what it means to be masculine, in the case of a man, or about what it means to be feminine for a woman. In other words, something that should be there is missing—this is the poverty or lack—and because the desire for love and affection remains, that desire understandably goes off track and inevitably leads to pain, disappointment, and even acute suffering...because there is a human nature that is a guide to right action.[44]

While Fr. Check's comments are specifically referring to homosexuals, this concept of mistaken identity, this same poverty, can apply to each and every one of us. We're all looking for love, fulfillment, and happiness. Fr. Check explains that we conform to what society tells us we should be in order to be accepted and loved instead of embracing our true identity as beloved children of God, made in his image and likeness.

> Our work, therefore, it seems to me, is to help people properly understand and sort through the appetites

> or attractions they have, and to separate noble and good desires from counterfeit ones. And to make those essential distinctions can only be successful if someone knows and believes in the personal dignity he or she has from God. Is this not what Christ came to show us?[45]

We fail to realize, can't quite grasp, or maybe haven't ever heard that we are loved not because of what we do or what is on the outside but because we are sons and daughters of God. As Fr. Check told a Courage gathering in Detroit:

> With specific regard to homosexuality, we can help people to see that their path in life is not reduced to only two choices: yielding to their inclinations for erotic contact with a member of the same sex and for the homosexual life on the one hand, or hiding in shame and fear, on the other. The Church offers another invitation, to authentic discipleship in Jesus and in chaste friendship with those on a similar walk to and with the Lord. But first, before we can guide them in how to live, we have to instruct them about who they are. Even at fifty-five, I am still growing in—or should be growing in—self-knowledge, about my true identity, with all that is good and a gift from God, and all that I have done to damage, in whatever measure, that gift. I imagine the same is true for you. The process is lifelong.[46]

When I lost my very prominent position in TV news, I mistakenly thought I had lost everything, including my identity. The secular world had convinced me that my career, and how successful that career was, determined my worth in my own eyes and everyone else's. I had no identity outside the newsroom; although I had been raised Catholic, those positive, healthy messages about God's love were drowned out by the much louder and more persistent voices of the world. Some of the confusion I faced—my own personal identity crisis—came from a very limited understanding regarding what it means to be a child of God. I knew I had a soul. I still called myself a Christian. But the life I was living spoke otherwise. My existence was based on only the physical and material; the spiritual element was missing, which explains why I felt so empty. It wasn't just about suddenly finding myself in the unemployment line. It was about how short-lived and conditional my self-worth had become.

Let's continue our refresher course on what it means to be made in the image of God. We can start with Genesis 1:27: "So God created humankind in his image, in the image of God he created them; male and female he created them."

If we are made in God's image, we can only be fulfilled and healed of our brokenness by putting him first in our lives. When we leave out the spiritual component, we are ignoring a very important part of who we are. And when we're not in relationship with God first, we try to fulfill that idea of communion or relationship in a variety of ways. For me and Sue Ellen, it was our careers.

A document released by the International Theological Commission (an important Vatican advisory panel made up of Catholic theologians from around the world), reflected on the writings and teachings of John Paul II based on his deep insights on the topic of *imago Dei* or "the image and likeness of God."

These reflections were introduced by the ITC at the turn of the twenty-first century when, thanks to scientific understanding and technical capabilities, society was experiencing an unexpected and possibly uncontrollable impact on the environment and the human race.

To put it more simply, the human race was beginning to doubt the truth of *imago Dei.* We were discovering just how immense and how old the universe was, and the knowledge gained made us question our own significance and our unique and sacred development. The ITC was trying to bring us back to square one, similar to what Fr. Robert Spitzer referred to as that "upward yearning."

> Created in the image of God, human beings are by nature bodily and spiritual, men and women made for one another, persons oriented towards communion with God and with one another, wounded by sin and in need of salvation, and destined to be conformed to Christ, the perfect image of the Father, in the power of the Holy Spirit.[47]

Fr. Paul Check says that the most important question ever asked in human history is a question of identity.

> "Who do you say that I am?" Jesus asked the apostles. That question leads to our confession that Jesus is Lord. But in a more general sense, the Master is teaching us that we must know ourselves, and others, in an honest and accurate way, with His love, mercy, and truth forming the light in which we can properly answer the question "Who am I?" We know that

> we cannot understand ourselves without reference to things outside of ourselves, like our family, for instance. How can I know who I am, if I don't know where I have come from?
>
> The philosophers say, *Agere sequitur esse*: "actions follow being." If I know this is a cell phone, then I know what it is for. To know what a human being is for, and so to know where the human person finds fulfillment, must be necessarily be preceded by answering the question, "What does it mean to be human?" Personal sincerity or "authenticity," while necessary and important, are not sufficient for me to be certain I am on the right path in a given instance, or more generally, as human experience reveals. I can make mistakes.[48]

Humans can and do make a lot of mistakes, and in these "anything goes" days, that includes making up their identity as they go along. A woman in Washington state made headlines in the summer of 2015 when her parents told the world her shocking secret. Even though Rachel Dolezal was working as the president of a local NAACP chapter and had passed herself off as an African American for years, in an interview with her biological parents (who are both white), they revealed that she is a white woman of European (not African) descent. Despite losing her job and causing a lot of people, including her family, friends, and members of the African American community much pain and confusion, she still clings to as much of her invented identity as she can. In interviews given months after the story broke, she still told reporters that she identifies herself as black.[49]

There is something much deeper going on in Dolezal than a mere interest in African American culture and history; to her, it was about her own identity. It was a struggle, and in the end, there was no denying her DNA, who she was created to be.

While our struggle was nothing like this woman's, Sue Ellen and I also ran away in one sense or another and we forgot who we really were. Like Dorothy in the children's classic, we created another identity as we looked for and landed in our own version of Oz. This make-believe existence that looked so beautiful and exciting on the surface eventually made us miserable. There is nothing wrong with having dreams for a better life. But those dreams need to be built on the reality of our human dignity, not on an empty idea from the culture or a false reality we've created on some social media site.

As Sue Ellen did, I found my true self by returning to my roots and taking my faith seriously, which is the only way to discover lasting peace and true joy. I discovered that there really is no place like home in the arms of Christ.

Come to the Quiet

Take a few minutes to meditate upon the following quote from Pope Francis at World Youth Day. Think about what he says in terms of our hunger for happiness. Think about the areas of your life that may be broken and the ways in which you have been trying to mend those wounds or stop the hunger pains.

> Dear friends, it is certainly necessary to give bread to the hungry—this is an act of justice. But there is also a deeper hunger, the hunger for a happiness that only God can satisfy, the hunger for dignity. There is neither

real promotion of the common good nor real human development when there is ignorance of the fundamental pillars that govern a nation, its non-material goods: *life,* which is a gift of God, a value always to be protected and promoted; *the family,* the foundation of coexistence and a remedy against social fragmentation; *integral education,* which cannot be reduced to the mere transmission of information for purposes of generating profit; *health,* which must seek the integral well-being of the person, including the spiritual dimension, essential for human balance and healthy coexistence; *security,* in the conviction that violence can be overcome only by changing human hearts.[50]

Time for Self-Reflection

- What spiritual dimensions are missing in your own life?
- How is your relationship with God? What are you hungering for?
- What practical steps might you take to grow spiritually?

—CHAPTER SIX—

A Picture Is Worth a Thousand Words—Then Again, Maybe Not

> Photography deals exquisitely with appearances, but nothing is what it appears to be.
>
> —DUANE MICHALS

Things aren't always as they seem, whether we're talking about yet one more self-edited selfie or something we see in a book, magazine, or on TV. And yet people continue to build their worlds around make-believe fantasies that don't actually exist. Listen to what Sue Ellen Browder has to say about how the "Cosmo girl" influenced women at the time:

> We wrote about this sexually "free" woman as if she really existed. Over time, readers who regarded the fantasy as real began to live out the Cosmo lifestyle. Within a decade or so, those of us who wrote regularly for the magazine began to find single women openly sleeping with their boyfriends everywhere, and I no longer had to make up so many anecdotes to produce an article Helen deemed publishable.[51]

This "sexually free woman" was a persona originally developed by author and former long-time *Cosmopolitan* editor, Helen Gurley Brown. Brown's book *Sex and the Single Girl,* published during the height of the sexual revolution, was a huge sensation and also the forerunner to the popular *Sex and the City* television series, which ran for years on cable. It all began with an idea introduced to the public in such a way that the public would not only embrace an agenda theoretically but buy into it as well.

In *Sex and the Single Girl,* Gurley Brown claimed that men think of a single woman "alone in her apartment, smooth legs, sheathed in pink silk Capri pants, lying tantalizingly among dozens of satin cushions, trying to read but not very successfully, for he is in that room filling her thoughts, her dreams, her life."[52]

As sexist as this description was, the public did buy it—hook, line, and sinker, as the old saying goes—to the tune of billions of dollars spent on various products related to a persona that was a complete piece of fiction, as was the "sexual revolution" that followed. "Splitting sex from babies spawned many lucrative new industries and would continue to do so as the decades rolled by and the sexual revolution juggernaut barreled down the tracks, crushing babies and families under and silencing anyone who dared to stand in its path."[53]

Cosmopolitan's circulation went from fewer than 800,000 to nearly 3 million copies, with annual advertising revenues jumping between 1964 and 1985 from about 600,000 to over 47 million.

Fast-forward to not just the "year of the selfie" but the "age of the selfie." We are living in an age where people are altering their images in order to look like other altered images in magazine spreads, on billboards in Times Square, and on social media. All of this for what purpose and to what end—to garner more attention, meet a significant other, and fulfill dreams of grandeur?

The rise of the selfie, for example, is having a huge impact on the demand for facial plastic surgery according to a statement from the American Academy of Facial, Plastic, and Reconstructive Surgery. AAFPRS president, Dr. Edward Farrior, said their annual survey finds that there is no denying that social media plays a part in the desire for plastic surgery, especially in the lives of young people. The study revealed:

- One in three facial plastic surgeons surveyed saw an increase in requests for procedures from patients who wanted to look better in social media.
- AAFPRS members surveyed noted a 10 percent increase in rhinoplasty in 2013 over 2012, as well as a 7 percent increase in hair transplants and a 6 percent increase in eyelid surgery.
- Image-based social platforms like Instagram, Snapchat, and Selfie.im have been identified as a driving force behind an increasingly youthful face of plastic surgery. In 2013, more than half of surveyed facial plastic surgeons (58 percent) saw an increase in cosmetic surgery or injectables in those under age 30.[54]

Why? Many young adults, viewing themselves on social media, are holding a microscope up to their own image and looking at it with a more self-critical eye, anxious about how they will be regarded by prospective friends, romantic interests, even employers. They want to put their "best face forward."

True Beauty?

This desire for outward perfection is nothing new, and it's something with which I am more than just vaguely familiar. Growing up in the early 1970s, we obviously weren't nearly as inundated with media messages the way we are today. But as Sue Ellen Browder points out, the cultural influences were still powerful enough to change attitudes, lifestyles, and beliefs (even the belief in something or someone that wasn't real).

Since I knew at a very early age that I wanted to pursue a career in broadcasting, I also realized that would mean being in front of a camera. As a young girl one of my favorite shows was the ABC TV sitcom, *The Partridge Family* (maybe you've caught a few reruns on cable). The plot was based around a single mom (played by Shirley Jones) who teamed up with her children to form a popular singing group. It was *the* hit show back then, and all the young girls, myself included, had a crush on Keith Partridge (played by David Cassidy), whose sister Laurie was played by Susan Dey.

Before becoming a star on *The Partridge Family,* Susan had a successful modeling career gracing the cover of *Seventeen* magazine and other fashion publications. Since just about every tween girl was head-over-heels for David Cassidy, every tween girl also wanted to look like Susan Dey. She was tall, extremely thin, with long, straight dark hair. I had the dark hair, but I wasn't thin by any means, having struggled with my weight since childhood. I thought if I could just be skinny like her, then maybe I would not only find a boyfriend as adorable as David Cassidy, but what the heck, it might help me fulfill my own dreams of being on television.

So I talked with my parents about going on a diet. My mom agreed to discuss it with the pediatrician at my next checkup. The doctor suggested that I cut out the sweets and snacks and lose no more than ten pounds or so. She gave my mom some dietary guidelines, and within a few short months, I had dropped about twelve pounds.

Accolades about my appearance flowed in from family and friends, and quite frankly I couldn't stop looking in the mirror. Despite the compliments I didn't think I was close enough to even resembling my skinny idol on TV, so I kept looking in the mirror, weighing myself, and dieting. Over the next three months, my weight dropped to about ninety pounds, and I found myself in Children's Hospital of Michigan. I was diagnosed with one of their first cases of a newly documented eating disorder: anorexia nervosa, which is marked by a fear of becoming overweight that leads to excessive dieting and extreme weight loss.

My Battle with Anorexia

Back in the seventies there wasn't all that much known about the causes of anorexia or its cure. A steady stream of doctors and psychologists visited my hospital room to ask me questions. Did I have control issues? Had I somehow been neglected emotionally by my parents? The answer I gave them then is the same answer I give now when asked about my struggles with anorexia: I just wanted to be skinny and look like a TV star because I thought it would make me happy and help me get what I wanted—a cute boyfriend and a career in broadcast journalism.

Although I didn't tell the doctors at the time, I had started to realize that, no matter how thin I was, I was never satisfied with the way I looked. When I stopped in front of a mirror, I still saw a chubby tween. In my mind I literally saw a completely different, imaginary view of myself, which is very common among anorexics. I had become very vain and extremely obsessed with my appearance. I can't even imagine what would have happened to me if I had access to the Internet or selfies. I'm sure it would have made matters much worse.

Sadly, today there are numerous websites and blogs that actively promote eating disorders. There is a growing group of people around the globe who actually call themselves "pro ana" (as in anorexia) and "pro mia" (as in bulimia) and embrace eating disorders as a lifestyle choice. They often proudly share their emaciated selfies to see how they rank against others in their weight loss category. They also compare notes, for example, on how to not eat for days at a time and how to prevent hair loss during starvation periods.

> This idea of community, of anorexics and bulimics feeling the need to "belong" to a virtual family, is played out across a number of the websites. On the world's largest pro-ana forum, which has 65,000 users and 1.5 million posts, many topics are available exclusively to members—with increasing layers of access granted the longer they stay with the site.[55]

I was in the hospital for a week. The doctors told me that if I wanted to go back to school, I would have to start eating again. Otherwise, they said, I would have to basically put life on hold in order to get healthy. That was enough to shock me back to reality and start eating again, although the effects of anorexia lingered for some time. Although I don't have any type of medical background nor have I studied psychology, in my own experience as an eating disorder survivor, I think the illness to some extent stays with you. Even today, decades later, I still have to stop myself on occasion from obsessing about what I am eating or how much I weigh. Part of this stems from the fact that I am still a public person and on TV so it's important to present a healthy image. But every once in a while, even with all of the research I have done on this issue and again my own experience, I still compare myself to someone on television or in a fashion magazine. The constant images from our culture telling us that if we're not a size "0" than we're obese, are everywhere.

Years later I was stunned to learn that all that glitters on TV (and everywhere else) is not always gold. My idol, Susan Dey, revealed to the public that while she was the sweetheart of the seventies on television, she was also struggling with both anorexia and bulimia.[56] Bulimia is a food disorder that involves frequent bouts of binge eating followed by purging, along with excessive use of laxatives and diuretics. Bulimia is often interrupted by periods of anorexia as well. According to the National Eating Disorders Association website, in the United States about twenty million women and ten million men suffer from some form of an eating disorder such as anorexia, bulimia, or binge eating. The NEDA says several social factors contribute to the problem:[57]

- Cultural pressures that glorify "thinness" or muscularity and place value on obtaining the "perfect body"
- Narrow definitions of beauty that include only women and men of specific body weights and shapes
- Cultural norms that value people on the basis of physical appearance and not inner qualities and strengths

The social and cultural pressures are growing stronger by the day, thanks to the explosion of media technology, with selfies no doubt being among the top culprits to contribute to this troubling phenomenon.

What I thought was a perfect appearance was only an illusion. I was modeling myself after another person struggling with not only one serious disorder, but two. Although I never became a Susan Dey lookalike, we had something else in common in terms of the fallout from our disorders. We were both so malnourished that we stopped menstruating. This caused problems for me later in life, which is one of the reasons I share such an embarrassing story. Maybe my battle with anorexia will help someone else think twice before he or she takes great risks in order to look like and live up to the often greatly modified images we see of the rich and famous every time they tweet, post, or pin the next latest and greatest selfie. On the bright side, Susan Dey and I both were able to overcome our challenges through support of our family.

Several years ago super model Cindy Crawford made headlines when she pointed out the woman in all of those glossy glamour shots barely resembles what she looks like in real life.

"I wish I looked like Cindy Crawford," she said.[58] Her comments caused a lot of buzz, but apparently given the popularity of selfie surgery, image-editing apps, not to mention the high rates of eating disorders, they didn't make much of a dent.

Quiz Time: Do You Like Your Body?

Do you like the way you look? Or, given the chance, is there something you would change about yourself? Let's take a closer look at that beautiful, confident woman in your bathroom mirror!

1. You see a friend's car pulling into your driveway unexpectedly. What's the first thing you do?
   a. Throw all the dirty laundry into the shower and pull the curtain shut.
   b. Put the tea kettle on and put your favorite mugs on the kitchen table.
   c. Hide. You just can't be seen in yoga pants!
2. You see a woman at church who is wearing a dress you have in your closet. What's your first reaction?
   a. Wow. It looks *so* much better on her than it does on me!
   b. Thank goodness I didn't wear mine!
   c. Oh, look. She must like that store, too!
3. If money was no object, on what part of your body would you like to "turn back the clock"?
   a. My cellulite—pretty much all over.
   b. I would like to get rid of all those gray hairs!
   c. I wouldn't change a thing.

How did you do? Don't worry if you're a little self-conscious at times about the changes that have happened to your body over the course of time. It's not a sin to want to look your best! Just be conscious of any negative self-talk that might creep into your thinking. After all, you are a precious daughter of God—and he thinks you are beautiful!

Looks Are Everything vs. the Real You

Because our culture is obsessed with appearances, it's easy to get caught up in placing too much attention on our physical looks. While we might not develop an eating disorder, most of us would like to lose weight, have a perfectly toned physique, whiter teeth, and so on. And while it's important to present ourselves well and look our best, we might not realize how focusing too much on these things leads to the sin of vanity.

Like many sins, vanity springs from insecurity. We worry about how we look in the eyes of others, and we constantly seek affirmation from them. We become unduly concerned about our appearance. This leads to being one-dimensional and shallow.

The antidote to vanity is authenticity. Being genuine means being yourself—not an imitation of someone else. We can learn a great deal about authenticity and not being sucked in to the world's standards from two men who lived during Jesus's day: St. Matthew and Zacchaeus. They were both wealthy tax collectors who learned to follow truth versus the illusions of the world.

St. Matthew was collecting taxes in Capernaum when Jesus called him to a different life. "As Jesus was walking along, he saw a man called Matthew sitting at the tax booth; and he said to him, 'Follow me.' And he got up and followed him" (Matthew 9:9).

Zacchaeus was also a tax collector. He had heard stories about Jesus, and when he learned that Christ was passing through the town of Jericho, where he lived, his desire to see Jesus was so strong that he ran past the crowds and climbed up a sycamore tree.

> When Jesus came to the place, he looked up and said to him, "Zacchaeus, hurry and come down; for I must stay at your house today." So he hurried down and

> was happy to welcome him. All who saw it began to grumble and said, "He has gone to be the guest of one who is a sinner." Zacchaeus stood there and said to the Lord, "Look, half of my possessions, Lord, I will give to the poor; and if I have defrauded anyone of anything, I will pay back four times as much." Then Jesus said to him, "Today salvation has come to this house, because he too is a son of Abraham. For the Son of Man came to seek out and to save the lost" (Luke 19:5–10).

Compare the spiritual journeys of these two disciples to that of the rich young man who could not walk away from his wealth, comfort, and the image of what he thought his life should be.

> As he was setting out on a journey, a man ran up and knelt before him, and asked him, "Good Teacher, what must I do to inherit eternal life?" Jesus said to him, "Why do you call me good? No one is good but God alone. You know the commandments: 'You shall not murder; You shall not commit adultery; You shall not steal; You shall not bear false witness; You shall not defraud; Honor your father and mother.'" He said to him, "Teacher, I have kept all these since my youth." Jesus, looking at him, loved him and said, "You lack one thing; go, sell what you own, and give the money to the poor, and you will have treasure in heaven; then come, follow me." When he heard this, he was shocked and went away grieving, for he had many possessions (Mark 10:17–22).

Matthew and Zacchaeus responded to the call of Christ. Deep down something clicked with them and they realized they were being deceived by worldly illusions of wealth and happiness. Zacchaeus, who was short in stature, must have had something tugging at his heart, because his desire to see Jesus was so strong that he climbed up a tree just to get a look at Jesus. He desired to see things differently. Apparently, so did St. Matthew—he just got up and walked away from his lucrative life as a tax collector.

By contrast, the rich young man's desire to be saved was not as strong as his view of the way he thought life should be. Jesus knew of his inner struggle, and that's why he told him that following the commandments wasn't enough. He had to be able to let go of what the world held for him. In his vanity and what he wrongly saw as security he walked away "disheartened and sorrowful."

Come to the Quiet

How can we enjoy the benefits of technology but still maintain our authenticity? How can we refrain from being caught up in how we look to others? In this book, I'm not advocating that we see social media as something bad. It's a powerful tool for connecting with others in ways that just aren't possible without it. But it's important for us to be able to see through the facade of worldly images and ideals. As followers of Christ, our desire should not be imitating what the world tells us is real and beautiful; instead, we want to see ourselves through the eyes of Christ. This is the face we can present to the world at large, whether that's sharing a selfie, blogging, or posting something on Facebook.

Time for Self-Reflection

In addition to spending time with the Scripture passages pertaining to St. Matthew, Zacchaeus, and the rich young man, reflect on this verse: "They [humans] look on the outward appearance, but the Lord looks on the heart" (1 Samuel 16:7).

- How have you allowed yourself to be deceived into thinking or believing something about yourself and God through social and cultural influences or outward appearances?
- Can you pinpoint a particular area of your life that has been affected by media messages or images that have been exaggerated or altered? What can you do differently in your life to grow closer to Christ?
- When you hear Christ's call, will you be able to walk away from whatever holds you back from following him the way St. Matthew and Zacchaeus did, or will you react more like the rich young man?

—CHAPTER SEVEN—

Perception Is Reality

The Problem with Seeing and Believing

> We know so little about one another.
> We embrace a shadow and love a dream.
>
> —HJALMAR SODERBERG

Think you're pretty savvy when it comes to not being misled by the mass media? Well, let's see if you can answer this multiple-choice question correctly: When Pope Francis uttered the now famous phrase "Who am I to judge?" he was:

A. Announcing his support of same-sex relationships
B. Changing Church teaching about same-sex marriage
C. Commenting on an alleged homosexual lobby at the Vatican

If you answered A or B, you would be among the majority—not only in the general public but also in the Church—who believe that Pope Francis's comments (made on an in-flight press conference on the way back from World Youth Day in 2013) were all about him giving a thumbs-up to active homosexual behavior and same-sex marriage. And just like all those other folks, you would be totally wrong.

The pope was actually answering questions about the status of an investigation regarding an alleged gay lobby at the Vatican and a monsignor who reportedly was connected to it. The pope said the investigation had come up empty, and then went on to use the moment to clarify Church teaching on the difference between same-sex attraction and active homosexuality.

Pope Francis reiterated the Church's belief that having a homosexual orientation is not sinful, unlike engaging in homosexual acts. "Who am I to judge a gay person of goodwill who seeks the Lord?" he said in response to a question about whether he would accept a celibate, homosexual priest in his diocese. "It [the *Catechism*] says they should not be marginalized because of this but that they must be integrated into society," he added, according to the BBC. The pope made his remarks as he addressed the possibility of a "gay lobby" within the Vatican, which has been the subject of discussion in the Italian press.

"There's a lot of talk about the gay lobby, but I've never seen it on the Vatican ID card!" he joked, according to John Allen of the *National Catholic Reporter*. "You have to distinguish between the fact of a person being gay, and the fact of a lobby," the pope told journalists.

"The problem is not having this orientation," the pontiff stated. "We must be brothers. The problem is lobbying by this orientation, or lobbies of greedy people, political lobbies, Masonic lobbies, so many lobbies. This is the worse problem."[59]

Once those five words (*Who am I to judge?*) were spoken, the secular press, gay activist groups, and others who have been waiting, hoping, and wrongly insisting that the Church was going to change its teaching on this core issue of marriage, took to the airwaves, the Internet, and social media in hopes of getting as many people as possible to believe the Church did something she could never do.

In many ways, the propagandists were successful. Ask the average Catholic if same-sex marriage has been approved by the Catholic Church, and more often than not, they would say yes and then most likely they would bring up the "Who am I to judge?" phrase as the reason for their incorrect answer. Even a number of my Catholic radio listeners—faithful people who are more knowledgeable about the Church, her teachings, and how she operates than most—were calling and e-mailing me, asking not *what* the pope actually said or did, but *why*. They should be among those that know better: Even if a pope wanted to change Church dogma, he can't. And even if a pope said he disagreed with a certain dogma or doctrine (which this pope never said), Church teaching would not and could not change.

Despite the fact that a quick search on the Internet would have led folks to the full transcript of the pope's inflight comments, and even though a few more clicks of the mouse would have led those who cared enough to the paragraphs 2357–2359 in the *Catechism* to which the pope was referring, most just accepted what the culture had put forth as gospel (no pun intended).

Social media has not only become "selfie central": a place for followers to share all kinds of photos, blurb, tweets, and posts about every detail of their lives, from what they ate or saw on television to what they did on their summer vacation. It's also become "news central"—or at least that's how certain media outlets want you to view it. Opinions on important issues are often shaped and formed by the kind of messaging we receive. The agents of information in some cases have an even stronger presence and following on social media than the standard outreach on-air or in print, and this enables their outlets to successfully help rally the troops on a number of hot-button issues.

Reflect again on the impact publications such as *Cosmopolitan* had on the lifestyle choices of generations of people. Sue Ellen Browder didn't have access to the Internet back then, and yet the fictitious "Cosmo Girl" went from fantasy to reality in a few short years. The perception was that a majority of women were Cosmo Girls, and so one by one countless others were convinced that they too needed to jump in the free-for-all pool.

Even if stories aren't "invented" as was so often the case with *Cosmo* and the other publications that helped propagate the sexual revolution, as receivers of information, we need to be aware of the media manipulation that occurs in an effort to sway public and personal opinion. That "opinion" is often the basis for important actions or behaviors. Opinion, however, is not the same as conscience, although it is often confused as such. The Catholic Church teaches that we need to have a well-formed conscience, and this doesn't mean getting swept up in popular social media commentary, hearing a few stories on the evening news, scanning the headlines, and then regurgitating sound bites—even though this is something that happens regularly.

> In the formation of conscience, the Word of God is the light for our path, we must assimilate it in faith and prayer and put it into practice. We must also examine our conscience before the Lord's Cross. We are assisted by the gifts of the Holy Spirit, aided by the witness or advice of others and guided by the authoritative teaching of the Church. (*CCC* 1785)

In frequent homilies, writings, and addresses, Charles J. Chaput, Archbishop of Philadelphia, reminds Catholics of the serious consequences of allowing ourselves to be convinced merely by cultural messaging and seeing conscience and opinion as one and the same.

> Each of us needs to follow his or her own properly formed conscience. But conscience doesn't emerge from a vacuum. It's not a matter of personal opinion or preference. If our conscience has the habit of telling us what we want to hear on difficult issues, then it's probably badly formed. A healthy conscience is the voice of God's truth in our hearts, and it should usually make us uncomfortable, because none of us is yet a saint. The way we get a healthy conscience is by submitting it and shaping it to the will of God; and the way we find God's will is by opening our hearts to the counsel and guidance of the Church that Jesus left us. If we find ourselves disagreeing as Catholics with the Catholic teaching of our Church on a serious matter, it's probably not the Church that's wrong. The problem is much more likely with us.[60]

The 2014 United States Religious Landscape study released by the Pew Center provides some pretty good evidence for the impact of the culture, or as Archbishop Chaput put it: Catholics disagreeing with Catholic teaching. The study shows that all major religious groups have become much more accepting of homosexuality.

> The number of evangelical Protestants, for example, who said they agreed that "homosexuality should be accepted by society" jumped 10 percentage points

> between the 2007 and 2014 studies—from 26 percent to 36 percent. The increase for Catholics was even steeper, from 58 percent to 70 percent. For historically black Protestant churches, acceptance jumped from 39 percent to 51 percent.[61]

If two supposedly savvy reporters such as Sue Ellen Browder and yours truly can be easily swayed, then why should we be surprised at how much stronger the cultural influence is on the average person?

It's not that Sue Ellen and I would expect someone who does not have a journalism background to know all the ins and outs of how stories are gathered and then disseminated. But one should have at least a general knowledge of how the media work, or else, as Archbishop Chaput says, the "the media will work on us." The archbishop, during a presentation in 2009 organized by the Pew Forum on Religion and Public Life, made a very strong and sobering point. Every day the mass media, not just the news media, are sending us a barrage of messages that most often conflict with our Catholic faith. If we are not aware of the agendas that could be behind the constant flow of emotional soundbites, headlines, or advertisements that glamorize or sympathize with actions contrary to the Gospel and more specifically to Church teaching, then we put ourselves in harm's way physically as I did with my eating disorder, or spiritually in terms of sin.

Quiz Time: Is It Hard to Be Catholic?

For two thousand years the Church has been proclaiming the truths of the Gospel received from Jesus and the apostles. Today, the moral teachings of the Church sometimes fly in the face of contemporary values. When you encounter this...how hard is it for you to accept and even defend the teachings of the Church?

1. When you see pictures of Pope Francis, you feel...
   a. Glad that he's the leader of the Church.
   b. Worried (or hopeful) that he is going to change essential Catholic teachings.
   c. None of the above.
2. Which of the teachings of the Church do you find hardest to reconcile with your own beliefs and values?
   a. Teachings about family life (contraception, abortion, reproductive technology, who is free to marry in the Church).
   b. Teachings about priestly life (who can be a priest or deacon, and the roles they play in the Church).
   c. Other social teachings (war, capital punishment, end of life issues, immigration).
   d. Other: ______________________.
3. When someone puts down or misrepresents what you believe, what are you most likely to do?
   a. Argue or complain.
   b. Ignore.
   c. Explain.

While it's true that not all those who consider themselves Catholic believe exactly the same thing that the Church teaches in its official documents, it's important to keep exploring and learning about the faith if we want our relationship with Jesus to grow. The beautiful thing about the Catholic faith is that there is a wealth of information that is readily available to anyone who wants to better understand what Catholics believe, and why. The *Catechism* is a great place to start—but once you start reading, you may discover that you are in for the (learning) adventure of a lifetime!

Being Light in a Culture of Darkness

"Jim" (not his real name) is a colleague of mine who works at a major metropolitan newspaper. He has been successfully employed as an investigative journalist at that same paper for over two decades. He is a devout Catholic, a man who is trying to maintain professional credibility in his work but admits it is getting more and more difficult for him to do so. He contacted me in the summer of 2015 shortly after the United States Supreme Court ruled in favor of same-sex marriage.

Jim says the public believes they are making decisions on key issues based on facts, and yet they have no idea how much they are being used—with the same-sex marriage issues being the ultimate example of this manipulation. He had a front-row seat to the propaganda push that went on behind the scenes. He watched his paper and countless other outlets do the same.

In the months preceding the Supreme Court decision on gay marriage, reporters were on the receiving end of a very slickly packaged public relations campaign to frame the issue before the court. Almost daily, they'd receive press releases, crafted by top-dollar firms based in New York, updating every turn of the screw in the case. The releases would be sent to any reporter whose name ever appeared on a story involving the case. You didn't have to be a federal courts reporter or a gay rights reporter to end up in the database of media contacts flooded with these releases.

The PR people would offer to arrange interviews with the litigants and their attorneys. They'd provide locations for the interviews so their clients could be photographed and filmed in the best light. They'd suggest "experts," mostly other lawyers, professors, and other academics, for reporters to interview on the subject.

In 2014, Bloomberg Politics ran an interesting graphic labeled "Newspapers prefer lesbians" showing how most newspapers that covered the case on the front page used women couples in their stories and photos. The graphic and the headline were interesting and provocative, but that was the end of it. No story. No questions to editors about the gender imbalance so evident on their front pages. No disgruntled male couples wondering why they were being left out. No polling data on the nation's comfort level with women couples versus men couples. Nope. Nothing to see here. A great chance to enlighten the public not only about gay marriage but about media coverage of it was wasted.

When Michigan Attorney General Bill Schuette litigated the gay marriage case in U.S. District Court, the public relations machine went into overdrive to discredit the witnesses called by the state, conducting what politicians would call "opposition research." Every witness brought to argue against gay marriage was dissected in the harshest possible light for the reporters. Press releases attacking the witnesses would fill up the inboxes of reporters, some of whom, sadly, repeated them without confirmation or even attributing from whence they came. None of this is illegal. Public relations practitioners have always sought to portray their clients in the best light and discredit people who oppose their clients.

The crime here is journalist malpractice. These reporters were being spun in the classic sense, yet they opened not their mouths, nor their eyes. The Michigan case involved two nurses from Hazel Park, a blue-collar suburb of Detroit. No reporters asked how they could afford the Harvard lawyers, the New York publicists, the travel, the interviews, and so on. Journalists, as Jim points out, should know instinctively to "follow the money," but this age-old adage never applied to the marriage issue.

It didn't occur to them that there could be a story in who was behind this effort to stagecraft this whole episode for public consumption. Nor did reporters recognize the imbalance. If you're being inundated by one side of a story, no matter how well financed, you still have a responsibility to seek out the other side, even if it doesn't magically appear in your inbox each morning. It's called reporting, which is not the same as stenography. But they didn't do that. Some of that is, no doubt, attributable to understaffed media outlets. But much of it is cultural. Reporters are supposed to be more circumspect than regular folks. But they can easily fall prey to the lazy notion of believing what they want to believe, no matter the facts.

Social media exploded the day the Supreme Court marriage decision came down. Avatars, e-mails, Facebook pages, all went rainbow-crazy that day. Photos of celebrations, rallies, and banners kept going viral with the majority of expressions supporting the Supreme Court decision. Emotions ran high, with millions getting caught up in the media frenzy. Even the president joined the party as the White House lit up in rainbow colors the night of the decision, marking the first time it was used to make a definite statement on a major controversial issue. I could fill another book documenting the type of steady propaganda that led up to gay marriage even becoming a possibility, but much of it was achieved by influencing the public to think that what they perceived on the surface was reality. People have a right to their opinions, but opinions should be formed on fact.

Follow the Money

While I never actually invented a story, I was certainly regularly pressured to do so, which is why I identify so closely with the experiences of Jim and Sue Ellen Browder. I quickly lost track of how many arguments I had with the promotions directors at the TV stations where I worked for so many years. Why, you might be wondering, would a news reporter be arguing with someone in promotions? Good question. The answer is that the news business, just like the magazine business, and the cosmetic and pharmaceutical industries, is just that: a business. Television stations will close their doors without advertising, and in order to sell advertising, it's necessary to have good ratings or high viewership. No used car salesman or department store owner wants to buy commercial time on a station that few are watching. The more viewers, the better the ratings and the higher the advertising rates—and that's where the promotions people come into play.

The promotions departments develop "promos" or "teases" to basically grab the attention of the viewers. In a world where so many outlets are competing for an audience, it's understandable that news departments make a concerted daily effort to entice those viewers. I got that—and I still get it. What I didn't get and still find utterly deceptive is an attempt by some in the industry to create a story before it happens. This is along the lines of what Sue Ellen experienced in her days at *Cosmopolitan*. Time and time again, a promotions department rep would inform me that he or she had already been teasing my story before I headed out the door with my camera crew.

It's one thing to promote a press conference or an impending strike, but to actually allow the creation of promos that claimed something had or would happen when we didn't know if that would be the case turned the news into nothing more than smoke and mirrors. Believe it or not, the powers that be would get upset with me for even suggesting that I actually be allowed to arrive at the scene of a story before we started making false claims based on what we hoped would happen for ratings sake. I suspect that the promotions department was often pressured by news executives and others in the front office, but I was never able to prove this.

One of the best examples of playing loosey-goosey with the truth comes from two close friends of mine: one a weatherman, the other an assignment editor regarding the same "story." Think back to the end of 1999 and all the fuss about the year 2000. It was something pretty special: being alive to see the turn of a century. The news media around the globe did its best to capitalize on the new millennium, and the TV stations in Detroit were no exception. Locally there were reports of a major storm moving in right after the New Year's holiday. That's when I received calls from both of my friends who worked at two different affiliates in the area. According to my buddies, they were livid with the stations' news management because they had received new information that the storm was changing direction.

The Detroit area was no longer in for piles of snow and ice, as earlier predicted. The storm to end all storms was being teased as the first major blizzard of the new century; "run for your lives, it's the end of the world" scenarios were all over the airwaves. As a result, schools, businesses, and government offices were shut down. Several major events had been cancelled. When the forecast changed, the promos still ran and the stations went with the story that was designed to alarm people as they hurried home from the crowded supermarkets with their cartons of milk and loaves of bread. Never let the facts get in the way of a good story! This is one of the reasons I eventually left the secular media. I simply got tired of banging my head against a brick wall for merely trying to do my job.

And so it continues. We make a variety of decisions, take drastic actions, and even live our lives based on what is often fiction instead of fact, which we allow to become our perception of reality. We're building a virtual house of cards. Indeed, we are too quick to believe appearances; our own or someone else's, even though very little is what it actually appears to be.

Blind Faith vs. Passionate Belief

As Catholics, we are meant to be "wise as serpents and innocent as doves" (Matthew 10:16). Unfortunately, too many of us, even though we are well-intentioned believers, accept what we see and hear in the media—even when it comes to our faith. To put it bluntly, we have become complacent, or even willfully ignorant. We have failed to question, investigate, and dig deeper; as a result, we end up jeopardizing our spiritual well-being.

To combat this, we can capitalize on the opportunity to learn everything we can about what the Church teaches about how to live in this world, but not of it. No spiritual laziness for us!

Instead, we can be concerned about our world and passionate about our faith. We can promote trustworthy news sources, whether print-based or digital. From radio TV shows to books and blogs, we can be part of reclaiming souls for Christ's kingdom.

But how do we know whom to trust when it comes to the media and their coverage of faith issues and in particular the Catholic Church? I think one of the best rules of thumb to establish is to take everything you hear in the secular press concerning the Catholic Church especially, with a huge grain of salt. It's not that all reporters necessarily have an agenda. But as you heard from my friend "Jim," many of them do. Even if they are just trying to cover a story few journalists are specialists any longer. In order to save money reporters are mostly general assignment. They cover a political campaign for a short time and then it's back on the general assignment beat where they cover everything from soup to nuts, so to speak. Most of the journalists who cover the pope, for example, do not have a deep grasp of Church teaching or Church operations. So it's always best to go to Catholic sources such as the Vatican website (www.vatican.va) as well as other well-known reputable sources such as EWTN and Ave Maria Radio which can be found at www.ewntnnews.com and www.avemariaradio.net.

Let's look at the example of Nicodemus in the New Testament. Nicodemus, a Pharisee, was fearful of meeting with Jesus. He was concerned that the same Jewish leaders who were plotting against Jesus, accusing him of all kinds of things, would become angry with him as well and cause trouble. He had the insider's track as to how the Pharisees and Sadducees felt about

Jesus because he was a Pharisee himself and a member of the Sanhedrin. While he had good reason to be worried, despite his fear he refused to blindly accept what the Sadducees and Pharisees were saying. He wanted to find out about Jesus for himself, and he wasn't afraid to take some risks to do so. He first met Jesus at night. Let's listen in on the surprising conversation he had with Jesus.

> Now there was a Pharisee named Nicodemus, a leader of the Jews. He came to Jesus by night and said to him, "Rabbi, we know that you are a teacher who has come from God; for no one can do these signs that you do apart from the presence of God." Jesus answered him, "Very truly, I tell you, no one can see the kingdom of God without being born from above." Nicodemus said to him, "How can anyone be born after having grown old? Can one enter a second time into the mother's womb and be born?" Jesus answered, "Very truly, I tell you, no one can enter the kingdom of God without being born of water and Spirit. For God so loved the world that he gave his only Son, so that everyone who believes in him may not perish but may have eternal life....
>
> "Indeed, God did not send the Son into the world to condemn the world, but in order that the world might be saved through him. Those who believe in him are not condemned; but those who do not believe are condemned already, because they have not believed in the name of the only Son of God. And this is the

> judgment, that the light has come into the world, and people loved darkness rather than light because their deeds were evil. For all who do evil hate the light and do not come to the light, so that their deeds may not be exposed. But those who do what is true come to the light, so that it may be clearly seen that their deeds have been done in God." (John 3:1–5, 16–21)

Nicodemus was forever changed by this encounter. When the members of the Sanhedrin wanted to put Jesus on trial, it's Nicodemus who boldly reminds them that Jewish law required a man to be heard before he was judged. Nicodemus later openly recognized Jesus and assisted in his burial.

Think about what Nicodemus would have missed had he believed what the Sanhedrin claimed to be true about Jesus. He could have just accepted their opinions and pronouncements and gone along with the program. Why upset the applecart? But he had a passion for truth and justice, and his persistence led him to God himself.

Come to the Quiet

Take some time to reflect on the following Scripture verses from the Old Testament and ponder the importance of both discerning the cultural messages of our day and doing our homework so we can live by Christ's message.

> My people are destroyed for lack of knowledge. (Hosea 4:6)

> Where there is no prophecy, the people cast off restraint, but happy are those who keep the law. (Proverbs 29:18)

Time for Self-Reflection

Think about how you process messages from the culture and reflect on the following questions:

- Do you stop at the tweets, Instagram posts, sound bites, and Facebook headlines, or do you take some time to search elsewhere in order to get "the rest of the story," as famous broadcaster Paul Harvey used to say?
- Do you typically accept what the media say about matters of faith, or do you seek out solid sources such as the various Vatican websites and Catholic media outlets?
- How has your faith been impacted by your complacency? Are you willing to make some changes?

—CHAPTER EIGHT—

Time to Refocus: What Are You Living For?

> Whoever serves and gives seems like a failure in the eyes of the world. In reality, it is exactly in giving their life that they find it.
>
> —Pope Francis

By all accounts and according to worldly standards, the Australian-born model Essena O'Neill had it made. She had built a career on social media, becoming an overnight Internet sensation with hundreds of thousands of followers and a nice chunk of change to the tune of several thousand dollars per selfie. With money and fame that went well beyond any nineteen-year-old's wildest dreams, what could possibly be missing?

Well, apparently everything. Referring to her former career as an empty and false life she created, in the fall of 2015 O'Neill shocked her more than *eight hundred thousand* followers on Instagram by suddenly launching a campaign *against* social media, changing her Instagram name to "Social Media Is Not Real Life." She recaptioned her online photos to show how they had been manipulated by technology. In one picture, clad in a bikini, the caption explained that the photo had been taken more than a hundred times. The caption reads, "There is nothing real about this."[62]

In an emotional video she recorded, O'Neill claimed that so many images of herself were repeatedly edited that she didn't even know what was real anymore. She recalled how quickly her selfies became an obsession for approval, and this consumed her.

> This was the reason why I quit social media: for me, personally, it consumed me. I wasn't living in a 3D world. I remember I obsessively checked the like count for a full week since uploading it. It got 5 likes. This was when I was so hungry for social media validation.... Now marks the day I quit all social media and focus on real life projects.[63]

She was brutally honest about constantly attempting to change her appearance, confessing that she obsessively restricted her calories and exercised excessively.

Some accused the teen of engaging in yet another marketing ploy: revamping her image to gain even more attention and media exposure. O'Neill, however, insists this is not the case; instead she is encouraging her followers to join her in living a real life in the real world. "Go outside, go to a park, go to a beach, go somewhere where there are people around you. What I am doing here is a statement that real life isn't through screens."[64]

Now she challenges her followers to try and go even a week without social media. In one of her videos, she says she hopes to convince as many people as possible that all that glitters is indeed not gold. She appeared to be the "pinnacle of success" but inside, she was miserable. "I had it all and I was miserable because when you let yourself be defined by numbers you let yourself be defined by something that is not pure, that is not real."[65]

By the world's standards she had everything to lose tells those who have not yet allowed themselves to be l selfie world that they have everything to gain.

> I'm not against social sharing. I am against the current status of social media and I have everything to lose by doing this. The majority of people seeing me do this on social media—you have nothing to lose. You have everything to gain. There are people around you. Go do things that you love to do in the real world.[66]

Although Essena O'Neill never brings up the issue of faith, the concepts she raises concerning making a difference echo what Jesus says about laying down our lives for others. She tells people to go out and volunteer, meet people, be connected. "You don't need to prove your value on social media."

A week after Essena O'Neill announced her plans to look for real meaning in her life outside of herself, Pope Francis told a congregation gathered at St. Peter's that focusing on the needs of others is completely countercultural, but it's the only way to find true happiness.

> Whoever serves and gives, seems like a failure in the eyes of the world. In reality, it is exactly in giving their life that they find it. A life that "takes possession of itself, losing itself in love, imitates Christ" in defeating death and giving life to the world, he said, adding that "whoever serves, saves. On the contrary, those who don't serve have no reason to be alive."[67]

The pope was celebrating Mass for the cardinals and bishops who passed away in 2015, and he stressed the sacrifices made by them as they lived their lives for the Church and not themselves.

> One's life ought to be spent imitating Jesus' example of humble service and self-giving, rather than focusing on one's own needs and interests. Jesus came not to be served, but to serve and give his life as a ransom for others—and he did it out of love. [The love of Jesus is] truly a concrete love, so concrete that he took our death upon himself.... This is the abasement that the Son of God underwent: bending down to us as a servant to assume everything that is ours, opening wide for us the doors of life.[68]

Pope Francis asked those sitting in St. Peter's that day the same question Essena O'Neill essentially asked the followers who were so enamored with her allegedly glamorous and fulfilling life: "What are you living for?"

All of us have to ask ourselves that question. What are we living for? Is what we're living for right now truly God's will for our lives? If it's not God's will, if you're honest with yourself, you'll eventually know it. St. Paul tells us in Romans 2:15 that "what the law requires" is written on our hearts.

Quiz Time: What Are You Living For?

When you think about your life, how do you feel about it? How do you think God feels about it? Take this quiz to explore the connection between faith and "real life."

1. As you go through each day, the predominant emotion you experience is...
   - a. Anxiety or stress.
   - b. Contentment or confidence.
   - c. Depression.
   - d. None of the above.

2. What did you do this week that has given you the greatest sense of joy and peace?
   a. Spending time with family and friends.
   b. Working (either paid or volunteer).
   c. None of the above.
3. Mother Teresa said that we are to do "little things with great love." Do you think this is. . .?
   a. The story of my life.
   b. An unrealistic but admirable goal.
   c. The reason she is a saint—and I'm not!

Depending upon how you answered these questions, you might be feeling as though you (like Essena) are in need of a change. Don't be afraid to make it! If you ask God to show you the right path, he is always faithful to show it to you.

When It's Time to Walk

Her followers, friends, and business associates were shocked when Essena O'Neill made such a radical change. Why in the world would she walk away from so much fame and fortune? Had she stayed in the spotlight, she stood to earn even more money. But it didn't make her happy. Something wasn't sitting right with her at the core of her being, in her soul, and she knew something had to change.

Some of my close friends and even some of my relatives thought I had a few screws loose when I decided to walk away from the secular media over sixteen years ago. It had been seven years since my return to the Catholic Church, and I was working as a news director for a large FM station in the Detroit area. It was a cushy job, to say the least. The money was great, and I had weekends and holidays off—which was a major coup in the 24/7 broadcasting business. In addition to being part of a popular daily morning drive radio show, I had my own weekend public affairs program. What could make me want to walk away from all that?

Well, while I wasn't as totally miserable and lost as Essena, I can certainly say that I wasn't fulfilled either. After leaving TV news in the late 1990s, I thought that going back to secular radio would be a great fit for me. It would provide me with regular hours and allow me to pursue some writing. My schedule was flexible enough that I could attend Bible study with my husband during the week and have somewhat of a normal life—much more normal than the grinding schedule of live TV news. I naively thought I could have at least some impact through my on-air work. There would be no more ambulance chasing; I no longer had to worry about doing live shots from horrible accident or murder scenes. I hoped I could be a positive influence and make some sort of a difference.

Within a few short months, I found out that the only difference the station owners were interested in was making was in the ratings. The bottom line was the only thing that mattered to them, and the only way to maintain that, in their minds, was to cater to the lowest common dominator—in others words, lots of trash talk, sexual content, and bad jokes. My time on the air was reduced to about two minutes of news per hour, consisting of mostly fluff or feature news stories. Yes, I was able to do some in-depth interviews on my public affairs program, but not really on the topics I cared about. In addition, the program aired on the weekends at the crack of dawn, so the only ones listening for the most part were Sunday morning golfers. Is this what I went to journalism school for?

As hard as it was for me to admit, the broadcast industry—and more specifically broadcast news—was hurtling down that slippery slope at high rates of speed, and I was going right down with it. I can identify to some extent with Essena O'Neil in terms of not being proud of the work I was doing. I started to feel ashamed to be associated with such weak and often foul programming content. Therefore, after only two years on the job, I approached my station manager and asked him to negotiate an early buyout for me. He agreed, and my husband and I used the money to start my communications and media awareness company.

In all honesty, in making this decision I struggled with my ego as I faced the loss of financial compensation and physical comfort of my radio news director's job. It wasn't as if I was the next Joan of Arc, was ready and willing to do anything to conquer the world for Christ. Far from it. For twenty years I had been a general assignment reporter in the rough-and-tumble world of TV news. That meant nights, weekends, holidays, early mornings. It meant standing outside in the brutal cold. Couldn't I just enjoy a cushy on-air job and coast for a while? I enjoyed being on the air and couldn't imagine my life without a microphone in it in some way, shape, or form.

But the law of the Lord, written on my heart, kept tugging at me, and deep down I knew I needed to move on. I knew I would never really be happy if I stayed in the secular media. I had no idea that I would someday be writing books, speaking, and hosting shows on Catholic radio and TV. I just knew that I wanted and needed to use my media skills for good. If I didn't, I would never be able to live with myself—no matter how appealing the perks were.

Superficial and Empty vs. Deeply Compassionate

The reality is that a shallow life—one lacking in depth and focusing on externals in hopes of finding personal satisfaction—just doesn't deliver. A truly meaningful life results from helping others, putting them before one's own comfort and satisfaction.

You might be surprised to learn that long before Essena O'Neill became an Internet celebrity, and long before yours truly jumped the secular media ship, the Christian concept of giving in order to receive, living for something other than one's self, had been proven successful—and not just in religious circles. Yes, compassion really does work when it comes to finding meaning, true joy. But wait; there's more. You also receive the added benefit of positively impacting the world around you and even improving your health. Who knew?

According to the Corporation for National and Community Service, recent studies show a strong relationship between volunteering and health. Those who volunteer, for example, live longer and have lower rates of depression compared to those who don't volunteer. Surprisingly, older volunteers receive the most benefits, perhaps because serving others provides them with a social outlet and keeps them physically active and healthier than their sedentary peers.

God is not some mean old ogre in the sky, just waiting to squash our fun. There is a reason people like Essena O'Neill decide there has to be more to life. There is a reason those who unselfishly serve others have a sense of fulfillment and tend to live healthier, happier lives. The reason is found over and over again in Scripture:

> Do nothing from selfish ambition or conceit, but in humility regard others as better than yourselves. Let

> each of you look not to your own interests, but to the interests of others. (Philippians 2:3–4)
>
> For where there is envy and selfish ambition, there will also be disorder and wickedness of every kind. (James 3:16)
>
> Then Jesus told his disciples, "If any want to become my followers, let them deny themselves and take up their cross and follow me. For those who want to save their life will lose it, and those who lose their life for my sake will find it." (Matthew 16:24–25)

So—what are you living for? Maybe it's time to change course. Don't forget that God always allows U-turns. He not only constantly encourages us to turn our lives around and come back to him, he offers to take over the driving. He is there to give direction, hope, and real meaning to our lives.

Think about the major U-turn King David had to make with his life. He was a powerful king who allowed himself to get puffed up and comfortable. He had an affair with another man's wife, the beautiful Bathsheba, and sent her husband to the frontlines of the battlefield, knowing full well he would be killed, thus enabling him to have Bathsheba all to himself. Now, if a murderer and an adulterer can become a "man after [God's] heart" (Acts 13:22), then I think there is a pretty good chance there is plenty of hope for the rest of us. God sent the prophet Nathan to challenge David, and eventually David came clean, repented, and became a great leader again.

St. Augustine of Hippo was also very familiar with U-turns. Don't laugh, but he is the patron saint of brewers because of his transformation from a worldly, sinful life full of partying and sexual escapades. He even had a child out of wedlock. All of those worldly pleasures, however, left him unfulfilled and restless. Once he found God he became one of our greatest Catholic teachers and is now known as a doctor of the Church.

Come to the Quiet

St. Augustine reminds us that we won't be truly happy unless we are living for God and not ourselves. Find some quiet time as you think about these words of his: "Our hearts are restless, Lord, until they rest in thee."

So put down that phone. Pick up your Bible and refocus. Take the advice of Fr. Robert Spitzer and look upward, and you just might find the answer to that important question: What are you living for?

Time for Self-Reflection

- How might you be feeling a sense of restlessness with your life right now?
- When is the last time you gave any thought to the question: What are you living for? How would you answer that question?

—CHAPTER NINE—

"Mr. DeMille, I'm No Longer Ready for That Close-Up"

The Importance of Finding Your Selfie Safe Zone

We live in a fantasy world, a world of illusion.
The great task in life is to find reality.

—Iris Murdoch

"Mr. DeMille, I'm ready for my close-up."[69] This famous line is from the classic film *Sunset Boulevard* starring Gloria Swanson as Norma Desmond, a faded silent film star who goes back and forth between reality and fantasy. If she is not dreaming of the days when her name was in lights, she is planning her big comeback—which never happens and was never going to happen. She engages an unsuccessful screenwriter looking for his first big break, a part played brilliantly by William Holden.

Desmond also gets her devoted servant to play along with the make-believe world of glitz and glamour that once filled her Hollywood mansion and her life. The servant happens to be one of her ex-husbands who is still so in love with the now aging starlet that he writes and mails fake fan letters to her and encourages her in her hopeless efforts to get back on the big screen. Both are so involved in the schemes that at times they believe them to be real.

The film is actually a flashback told by "Joe," who chronicles the developments in their tormented relationship that lead to his eventual ruin. It ends sadly with Holden's character deciding he has had enough of being controlled by Desmond. When he tries to leave after telling her she has long been forgotten and will never have that comeback, she shoots him. In the final scene the flashback is now over. We see the body of Joe and Desmond's home filled with news reporters and police officers that showed up after learning of the murder. Nora Desmond tragically mistakes the flashing lights of the police cars and reporters' cameras for the lights of the movie cameras. She believes she is back in the studio along Sunset Boulevard with that comeback about to begin. Staring straight ahead with a dazed and glazed look in her eyes, she says emphatically, "Mr. DeMille, I'm ready for my close-up."

The movie is a tragic story of a troubled woman who loses her identity when her movie career ends. It's an identity crisis so severe that the character had to create an alternate universe. Films like this might affect each of us differently, depending on our own efforts to replace reality with fantasy. For some it might be a wake-up call that helps them become more aware of their own attempts to get lost in a virtual, self-absorbed world. The film shows how easily others can be drawn into a world of make-believe in an effort to try to make their own existence more exciting. Others might just shrug their shoulders and comment on how the film, as entertaining as it is, is nothing more than a story of an aging, frustrated, and deranged actress. Something like that could never happen to stable people in real life.

Even though the film was released more than sixty-five years ago, there are some real modern-day lessons to be learned. If we look at the current headlines, there are plenty of examples of people—some of them in pretty sophisticated positions—who most likely never thought they would ever find themselves caught up in such delusions of grandeur.

Does the name Anthony Weiner ring a bell? He was a successful politician, a young New York congressman who was going places in the Democratic Party until a selfie sex scandal became his undoing. He actually was involved in two sex scandals revolving around illicit selfies he took and then texted (or sexted). The first scandal in 2011 involved a twenty-one-year-old woman who was on the receiving end of the photos, and it led to his eventual resignation from the House of Representatives.

The second scandal occurred just two years later as he was trying to make a political comeback as a candidate for New York City mayor. You might think Weiner would have learned his lesson. Instead he continued taking lewd photos of himself, and this time around it involved not one, not two, but *three* women. (Not all that unlike the fictional main character in *Sunset Boulevard,* who lured others into her web of lies and make-believe.) In Weiner's case, which happened to be real life, one wonders how such a prominent man with so much at stake could take such risks with his reputation, his marriage, and his career—not once, but twice, in a few short years.

In 2014 popular actress and model Jennifer Lawrence graced the cover of just about every magazine, was the lead story on every entertainment program, and became the top trending item on Twitter and other social media sites for all the wrong reasons. Her cell phone was hacked and the nude or semi-nude selfies she took were suddenly available for the entire world to see. In an exclusive interview a few months after the story originally broke, she told *Vanity Fair* she had no reason to apologize and nothing to be ashamed of.

> Just because I'm a public figure, just because I'm an actress, does not mean that I asked for this. It does not mean that it comes with the territory. It's my body, and it should be my choice, and the fact that it is not my choice is absolutely disgusting. I can't believe that we even live in that kind of world.... It is not a scandal. It is a sex crime. It is a sexual violation. It's disgusting. The law needs to be changed, and we need to change. That's why these web sites are responsible. Just the fact that somebody can be sexually exploited and violated, and the first thought that crosses somebody's mind is to make a profit from it. It's so beyond me. I just can't imagine being that detached from humanity. I can't imagine being that thoughtless and careless and so empty inside.... Anybody who looked at those pictures, you're perpetuating a sexual offense. You should cower with shame. Even people who I know and love say, "Oh, yeah, I looked at the pictures." I don't want to get mad, but at the same time I'm thinking, I didn't tell you that you could look at my naked body."[70]

Miss Lawrence has been the current Hollywood "it girl" for a few years now, and her stardom has led to numerous lucrative contracts with top cosmetic companies. Unlike poor Nora, Lawrence is obviously still a household name. For whatever reason, she was convinced the photos would help cement a long-distance relationship.

> I started to write an apology, but I don't have anything to say I'm sorry for. I was in a loving, healthy, great relationship for four years. It was long distance, and either your boyfriend is going to look at porn or he's going to look at you.[71]

I could write several chapters on how and why a young woman at her level of success believes she needs to send suggestive photos to her boyfriend in order to keep his interest. I could fill several other chapters with an examination of why the hacking certainly was a scandal, especially for young women who see her as a role model.

But in this chapter we're focusing on the sheer lack of common sense exhibited by two very prominent people who should know better. Politics and acting are among the most competitive professions going. Given the 24/7 media frenzies that build around politicians and Hollywood superstars and make for juicy copy and titillating photo spreads, what happened to Weiner and Lawrence's internal warning systems? Why wasn't the possibility of being caught or being exposed on their radar?

And therein lies the problem. If this can happen to Anthony Weiner and Jennifer Lawrence, two people who should be aware of the risks given their status, what does it say for the average person with a cell phone? All the more reason for you and your loved ones to find what I call the "selfie safe zone."

While Lawrence and Weiner weren't delusional like poor Nora Desmond, there was some level of denial and fantasy going on, combined with a certain level of arrogance and disconnect—or at the very least an extremely naïve approach to their involvement with technology. Today's technology can cause something to go around the world virally in less than a split second. How Anthony Weiner and Jennifer Lawrence could put that aside is the $50,000 question—a question that I hope will lead all of us to take the idea of a selfie safe zone more seriously.

Quiz Time: Are You in the "Selfie Safe Zone"?

When the media is concerned, the boundary between reality and fantasy can quickly become blurred. Do you know how to keep yourself and those you love safe?

The questions in this quiz are more of essay than multiple choice. It's an opportunity for you to think about (and talk with your husband or trusted friend about) these issues as they affect you and your family.

1. If you knew that a friend or adult daughter was toying with the idea of taking a "sexy selfie," how would you advise her?
2. What would you do if you found your husband or son was viewing sexually explicit materials? How does this kind of "fantasy" affect human relationships?
3. Have you ever known someone who has experienced identity theft? What would you do if you discovered someone had stolen your personal information?

Getting in the Zone

Being morally and legally responsible with technology may seem pretty obvious. But given all the examples of carelessness and cluelessness out there, the guidelines are golden rules worth repeating and sharing. They are also easily applied to a variety of age groups, from children to adults.

Sending and receiving sexually explicit materials (whether photographs or selfies) depending on the age of the senders and receivers, can be illegal. While the situation may vary from state to state, this type of exchange—commonly referred to as "sexting"—has been at the center of a number of major news stories in recent years involving young offenders. In 2014 two middle school boys from Chicago, for example, were arrested after police discovered sexually explicit pictures on their cell phones. They allegedly sent pictures to other students and were charged with trafficking child porn. And lest you think this can't happen in your family, 20 percent of high school students ages fourteen to eighteen admit to sexting, along with more than 25 percent of college students.

According to the Catholic Church pornography is an intrinsic evil. The *Catechism* teaches:

> Pornography consists in removing real or simulated sexual acts from the intimacy of the partners, in order to display them deliberately to third parties. It offends against chastity because it perverts the conjugal act, the intimate giving of spouses to each other. It does grave injury to the dignity of its participants (actors, vendors, the public), since each one becomes an object of base pleasure and illicit profit for others. It immerses all who are involved in the illusion of a fantasy world. It is a grave offense. Civil authorities should prevent the production and distribution of pornographic materials. (CCC 2354)

In the late 1990s a popular Christian slogan made the rounds and eventually ended up on wristbands and posters, asking the question, "What Would Jesus Do?" (best known as "WWJD") Taking that slogan and applying it to modern-day social media activities is a helpful Holy Spirit nudge that keeps us accountable. What would Jesus text? What would Jesus tweet? What kind of selfie would he take?

Pope Francis has the highest number of Twitter followers in the world. We've seen him pose for plenty of selfies with Catholics of all ages during his papal audiences and during his travels. Taking selfies can be a good and a wholesome thing and can even promote the joy of the Lord. It's all in the intent and the approach. Looking at selfies through the lenses of faith and the eyes of Christ will keep us grounded morally, spiritually, and legally as well.

Not keeping up with the Joneses (or those Kardashians!) is another way to establish and maintain a safe selfie zone. So what if the neighbors and all of their children have their own iPhone, iPad, iPad Mini, and enough tech toys to make their living room look like a scene from the latest *Star Wars* movie? That doesn't mean you have to plop the entire Internet world into the hands of your family members.

If you want your younger children to have cell phones for safety reasons, contact your carrier. All cell phone providers offer packages with plenty of parental controls. You can control how much, if any, Internet access your kids have. You can also limit the amount of texting and monitor their behavior from your own devices. And don't buy into what the Joneses might be saying about "trusting" their children. Tell Mr. and Mrs. Jones they need to face facts—as in medical facts. The frontal lobes—the portion of the brain that help children, tweens, teens, and even college students decide if a particular action may have consequences, aren't actually developed yet. This portion of the brain helps us weigh outcomes, form judgments, and control emotions and impulses. Since this area of the brain is not fully developed until a person is in his or her early twenties, what are parents thinking when they hand little Johnnie or Susie a device that connects them 24/7 to the wild world of the web?

One of the best media awareness organizations, Parents TV Council, offers a practical action-item list for dealing with all the messaging that floods our daily lives. This list is in the form of media resolutions for families. In an early 2016 article entitled "5 Media Resolutions for the New Year," Melissa Henson, the PTC director of Grass Roots Education and Advocacy and a frequent guest on my radio program, suggests that one of the best ways to deal with the media issues affecting both you and your children is for families to address media challenges together. This adds to the overall accountability factor. If children know Mom and Dad are paying close attention to what they're watching on TV or seeing online, they will be conscious of their own choices and more comfortable in talking with their parents about those choices. It is a lot easier to address an issue if parents establish regular and open dialogue. I'm sure there are at least one or two of these resolutions that, if applied, could make a real difference in all of our homes. Here are Henson's five resolutions:[72]

1. **Watch, listen, and play with your kids:** Most children spend more time with media than with any other socializing influence outside of school—that includes parents. If you want to play a role in helping your child develop his or her value system, you must engage while you have time, before the media he or she is consuming has the last say. Sharing media with your children

(watching TV with them, listening to the music they listen to, playing video games with them) is not only a good way to fully understand the messages your child might be exposed to, but it's also the best way to mitigate against any potentially damaging or harmful messages in the media they are consuming.

2. **Cut back:** Help your kids go on a media diet. Make and enforce media-free times. No cell phones during dinner, for example, or after 8:00 PM. Set up a family game night so that you're spending time together away from the television. Use the weekends to go on hikes, or ride bikes, or take a camping trip. Time spent with you and away from screens will be far more meaningful to your child in the long run.

3. **Make it count:** Not all screen-time is created equal. It is increasingly the case that kids have to spend a certain amount of time on computers or tablets in order to do their assigned schoolwork. Time spent Skyping with a parent deployed overseas is an unqualified good. Likewise, time spent on Minecraft or learning how to code; or on some creative endeavor like editing videos or writing for a blog; or with educational programs like Khan Academy or Rosetta Stone should not be viewed in the same way as purely passive activities like watching television. Don't make media the enemy; make it count.

4. **Support quality programming:** It has been rightly said that you "vote with your remote." It's not enough just to say you wish to see more family-friendly TV if you don't watch it when it is offered. There is ample evidence that network executives are motivated by more than just profits. Some insist on putting more of the content *they* want to see on air, regardless of what

viewers at home want. Yet if we don't support family-friendly programs when they *do* offer them, you can bet they won't waste any time pulling them from the schedule and replacing them with more sex and violence-laden programming. There are a handful of family-friendly cable networks out there that cater to family audiences with wholesome programming. Support those networks, and more importantly, support the sponsors who are helping to underwrite family-friendly content.

5. **Make your voice count:** If the executives and advertisers dumping degrading, demeaning, and damaging media into the marketplace aren't hearing back from you, they are going to assume you're just fine with what they're doing. By default, you are tacitly agreeing to their agenda. If you see something that you think doesn't belong on TV, Henson urges, "Contact the sponsors, contact the networks, and contact your broadcast affiliate or your cable company. You can find tools and resources to take action at www.ParentsTV.org. You can also sign up to receive regular e-alerts so that you can stay informed and involved. Don't wait for others to speak for you. Resolve this year to make your voice heard."

Even if you don't have children, Henson's resolutions deserve a closer look. You might even consider inviting some of your friends to join you in putting them into practice. You can do yourself a lot of good by getting your own media habits under control. Why not limit selfies, for example, to those that are very unique and meaningful? A photo op with the pope comes to mind, but if that's not in your future any time soon, reserve taking selfies with dear friends and loved ones for special occasions, such as a birthday or graduation party or a wedding.

Say so long to selfies at the gym, the mall, and the silly, senseless ones in front of your fridge or in line at the grocery store. The less time you spend taking selfies, the less time you'll spend posting, tweeting, and thinking only yourself. Such a decision might even result in time for other activities such as prayer and actual "face time" with family.

More, More, More vs. Enough Is Enough

If all else fails and you're tempted to snap one more selfie at the sushi bar, think of Norma, Anthony, and Jennifer. Isn't it better to be safe in the selfie zone than sorry? After all, one less close-up can't hurt. It could only help. You'll be developing one of the strongest spiritual muscles: self-control. And this is a virtue that sets in motion a positive cycle; self-control in one area leads to an ability to say when enough is enough in other areas. This virtue is sadly lacking in our culture, and thus it's a great way for you to shine the light of Christ into the darkness.

The apostle Paul is someone who struggled with temptation and learned self-control to overcome it. In 2 Corinthians 12 he talks about having a thorn in his flesh. He does not provide details of what this thorn is, but we get the impression that it is either a strong temptation to sin or a physical ailment—or maybe even both. St. Paul turns it into a Romans 8:28 situation ("all things work together for good"): This temptation or affliction is a constant reminder of his need for Jesus and the self-control to overcome it.

Come to the Quiet

The Catholic Church has an incredible body of teaching regarding media usage. OK, maybe, like a lot of folks, you're very busy and don't relish the idea of having to pore over various Vatican documents. I would strongly recommend, however, reading a few of the short but very insightful World Communications Day statements which can all be found at the main Vatican website (vatican.va).

Popes have been releasing these gems since the Second Vatican Council. A new one is released each year in January on the feast day of St. Francis de Sales, the patron of journalists. The World Communications Day itself for that year is held in May. These statements are relatively short, but they provide important lessons for Catholics on a variety of media topics, focusing on the ways Christians should be engaged in the media and how the media impact our lives and, most importantly, our faith journey.

One of my favorites is the 2011 World Communications Day statement issued by Benedict XVI and entitled *Truth, Proclamation, and Authenticity of Life in the Digital Age*. The document was written just about the time selfie craze was gathering steam. Use this Call to the Quiet to slowly read and ponder a few of the profound insights Benedict provides concerning our involvement in social media. Think about how his words correspond to concerns and issues raised in this book.

> Entering cyberspace can be a sign of an authentic search for personal encounters with others, provided that attention is paid to avoiding dangers such as enclosing oneself in a sort of parallel existence, or excessive exposure to the virtual world. In the search for sharing "friends" there is a challenge to be authentic and faithful and not give it to the illusion of constructing an artificial profile for oneself.

> The new technologies allow people to meet each other beyond the confines of space and of their own culture, creating in this way an entirely new world of potential friendships. This is a great opportunity but it also requires greater attention to and awareness of possible risks. Who is my neighbor in this new world? Does the danger exist that we may be less present to those whom we encounter in our everyday life? Is there a risk of being more distracted because our attention is fragmented and absorbed in a world other than the one in which we live? Do we have time to reflect critically on our choices and to foster human relationships that are truly deep and lasting? It is always important to remember that virtual contact cannot and must not take the place of direct human contact with people at every level of our lives.[73]

Time for Self-Reflection

Read 2 Corinthians 12:7–10. How can you be more like St. Paul and use your media temptations to bring you closer to Christ? St. Paul didn't let his "thorn in the flesh" separate him from Jesus; in fact, it had just the opposite effect. How about you? If you're having a hard time controlling your media usage, take it to the Lord in prayer and ask how this challenge can be used for good.

— CHAPTER TEN —

The Big Picture

How Changing Those Selfie Habits Just Might Change You and the World around You

> As the family goes, so goes the whole nation, and the world in which we live.
>
> —Pope St. John Paul II

We are all part of a family, and not just our physical family. We are part of the family of God. That's why our choices and actions have a huge ripple effect, even in our own little corner of the world where we think no one notices. Bad choices can cause our downfall, but depending on the severity of those choices, they can also have long-term and far-reaching effects beyond our homes and neighborhoods. That's why it's important to zoom out and take a look at the big picture—this reminds us of how we are all very much tied together. We need to connect the dots.

Too often in our morally relativistic culture, people can easily develop the mindset that it is all about choice. You choose what you want to do with your life, your time, your personal opinions, and I'll choose what I like. Choices, however, have consequences that can and do touch us—and those around us—in positive or negative ways. It's similar to what happens when we throw a pebble or stone into a pond. There is a definite ripple effect, which is what Pope St. John Paul II was getting at when he said, "As the family goes, so goes the whole nation and the world in which we live."

To gain a deeper appreciation of this ripple effect, let's take a look at some recent and very strong research that shows how strong families have a positive impact on society. Researcher W. Bradley Wilcox is a sociologist from the University of Virginia and a frequent guest on my show. He coauthored a 2015 report, *Do Healthy Families Affect the Wealth of States?* Released in the fall of 2015 through the University of Virginia and the American Enterprise Institute, it showed that states with higher levels of marriage, especially married spouses with families, are strongly associated with:

- More economic growth
- Less child poverty
- Less violent crime
- Higher median family income

According to the report, strong families often serve as seedbeds for the kind of virtues—such as a strong work ethic and the capacity for delayed gratification—that success in a vibrant free market requires. "Growing up in intact, two-parent homes makes children, especially boys, more likely to avoid disciplinary problems and stay on track in school, and makes both young men and women more likely to be gainfully employed later in life. Young adults often access job opportunities through family networks—again, especially if they come from intact, two-parent families. In other words, families help to supply the human and social capital that undergirds successful free-market economies in today's world."[74]

Think about the fallout from the Anthony Weiner scandal mentioned in the previous chapter. His choices didn't only impact him. His wife, his family, and his friends were negatively affected as well, not to mention the impact his actions had on the women with whom he was involved. And what about the voters who put him in office and the taxpayers that paid his salary? The reputation of his office or congressional seat was also tarnished, striking yet another blow to an already negative view of politicians. All of this stemmed from some really self-centered—or shall we say, "selfie-centered"—choices.

No pun intended, but are you getting the picture? Weiner is just one real-life example. But let's not forget all the tragic cases where people young and old lost either their lives or limbs by trying to grab the ultimate selfie. Think about the loss to their loved ones. Think about how many new programs and policies have been put in place at tourist attractions or amusement parks in order to prevent other tragedies. Think about the lives of those middle school boys in Chicago who faced charges because of a sexting scandal—how many people did they impact with their selfie stunts?

Let's zoom out even further and take a look at the mounds of evidence connecting too much media usage to a long list of societal ills. Of course, we can't blame the media for all of our problems—but we can't ignore it either. For dozens of years, medical experts, professional organizations, universities, and think tanks have generated study after study on media influence.

More recently, due to the prominence of social media, researchers are beginning to rack up even more studies on the impact selfies, tweets, and so on have on our relationships. The Pew Research Center's report entitled *Couples, the Internet, and Social Media* came out in February 2014. According to the survey of nearly twenty-three hundred adults eighteen and older, while technology can be beneficial in helping couples communicate as well as manage day-to-day activities, there is a real down side to technology as well, including:

- 25 percent of cell phone owners in a marriage or partnership felt that their spouse or partner was distracted by his or her cell phone when they were together.
- 8 percent of Internet users in a committed relationship have had an argument with their spouse or partner about the amount of time one of them was spending online.
- 4 percent of Internet users in a committed relationship have gotten upset at something they found out their spouse or partner was doing online.
- 10 percent of Internet users who are married or partnered say the Internet has had a "major impact" on their relationship.
- 17 percent say it has had a "minor impact."
- Fully 72 percent of married or committed online adults said the Internet has "no real impact at all" on their partnership.
- 74 percent of the adult Internet users who report that the Internet had an impact on their marriage or partnership say the impact was positive. Still, 20 percent said the impact was mostly negative, and 4 percent said it was both good and bad.

However, other studies show that a much more negative trend is occurring with social media causing issues in marriages. A 2014 study published in the journal *Computers in Human Behavior* found a correlation between social media and divorce rates in the United States. According to their research, a 20-percent hike in Facebook annual enrollment was associated with increased rates of divorce. The researchers also hypothesize that social media's addictive qualities may "create marital strife, promote an environment rife with opportunities for jealousy, and may help facilitate extra marital affairs."[75]

This isn't exactly rocket science, but sometimes when we've already established certain media patterns, we might be oblivious to the effects and not realize that change is required before it's too late. It's all about hitting that zoom button on the lens of our life and getting a broader look at what's really going on.

Unfortunately, a similar negative fallout can occur with children and the media, especially in terms of health issues including weight, sleep, behavior (prone to violence), and overall psychological well-being.

Quiz Time: Is Social Media Hurting Your Family?

In this last quiz, let's take a look at the big picture of social media and how your family's habits could be either enhancing or harming your communication.

1. It's dinner time! Where are your cell phones on most days?
   a. Fork in one hand, cell in the other. (How else can we let the whole world know what gourmet cuisine we are eating?)
   b. Middle of the table. First one to take a call has to do the dishes.
   c. Cell phones? We don't have no stinkin' cell phones!
2. How much time does your family spend together screen-free (no phones, computers, tablets, or television)?
   a. At least one hour per day, around dinner time.
   b. We tried this for Lent last year. Never again.
   c. We try to take at least a couple of hours every weekend.
3. What's the most common way for you to find out what's going on in each other's lives?

a. Facebook, baby. Or we text each other throughout the day.
b. While driving in the car. If I can yell past their earbuds.
c. At bedtime.

What could your family be doing to use social media more intentionally, and to be more personal in how you connect with one another? How often do you write notes, play board games, or simply set aside your devices and go for a walk? What is social media for you—a tool, or a trap?

The Pornography Trap

We haven't even touched on the problem with Internet pornography. If you talk to any Catholic priest, he will tell you the most common sin he hears in the confessional is connected to pornography usage and addiction.

In 2014, Bishop Paul S. Loverde of Arlington, Virginia, updated and reissued a powerful letter he wrote on the plague of pornography, "Bought with a Price: Every Man's Duty to Protect Himself and His Family from Our Pornographic Culture."

> In my nearly 50 years as a priest I have seen the evils of pornography spread like a plague throughout our culture. What was once the occasional vice of a few has become the mainstream entertainment for many—through the Internet, television, smart phones, and even portable gaming and entertainment devices designed for children and teenagers. Never before have so many Americans been tempted to view pornography. Never before have the accountability structures—to say nothing of the defenses—which every society must

> build to defend the precious gift of children—been so weak.[76]
>
> This plague stalks the souls of men, women, and children, ravages the bonds of marriages, and victimizes the most innocent among us. It obscures and destroys people's ability to see one another as unique and beautiful expressions of God's creation, instead darkening their vision [and] causing them to view others as an outlet for free expression, supported as a business venture, and condoned as just another form of entertainment.

The American Society of Addiction added pornography to their list of addictions a few years ago. Pornography has been mainstreamed on television and elsewhere through more and more sexuality explicit programming, and this adds to more desensitization. We begin to see it as the new normal. Take another look at Jennifer Lawrence's comment about her nude selfies that were released by hackers: "Either your boyfriend is going to look at porn or he is going to look at you."

It is so commonplace that even a stunning actress is convinced she has to lower herself to sexting her boyfriend in order to keep him in the relationship. Experts have also identified a "fantasy versus reality" component among porn users, with men expecting their wives or girlfriends to look exactly like the women in pornographic films. Their unrealistic expectations lead to relationship problems and sometimes divorce or breakups.

Fighting Spiritual Myopia

These findings are just the tip of the proverbial iceberg when it comes to the connection between media habits and how they impact us individually and our relationships. At first, the idea that changing our selfie-centered habits could change not only us but the world around us might sound far-fetched. However, it's a fact that strong families are better for a state's economic stability. Strong families are built on stability, love, sacrifice, mutual understanding, and we hope, deep faith. Our lives are much better, and true happiness is only found through living those same virtues.

It's tough, however, to build happy, strong individuals and families with high character if those individuals and families are overly focused on their tech toys, which all too often weaken rather than strengthen personal fulfillment and vital family bonds.

It was the lure of fame, fortune, and a false promise of fulfillment that caused a social media sensation to walk away from a fake life she built for herself on the Internet. In my case, it was media messaging that started me on a very rocky road that nearly cost me my marriage and more importantly my soul. It's clear that the effects of our "me, my selfie, and I" media habits can be compared to the long tentacles of an octopus, ready to suck the life out of all of us if we're not careful.

St. John Paul II had a very clear vision of the very big picture; he went against the "it's all about me" grain, instead reaffirming that no man is an island unto himself. It's all about you, me, us, them: the entire human race. The difference is significant. An "all about me" attitude results in spiritual myopia, which means seeing the world only from our own point of view, filtered through our own concerns and needs. We become shortsighted, with a lack of intellectual insight.

The antidote to spiritual myopia is *empathy.* No longer fixated on ourselves, we begin to see clearly around us. We become attuned to what our neighbors are dealing with, responding with empathy and interest rather than apathy and indifference.

The parable of the Good Samaritan, one of the most familiar—and also among the most touching and challenging—parables in the Gospels, features both types of responses. A lot of us would hardly blame those who passed by the injured man on the road to Jericho. How many times have we ignored someone in need because he or she looked dangerous?

> A man was going down from Jerusalem to Jericho, and fell into the hands of robbers, who stripped him, beat him, and went away, leaving him half dead. Now by chance a priest was going down that road; and when he saw him, he passed by on the other side. So likewise a Levite, when he came to the place and saw him, passed by on the other side. But a Samaritan while traveling came near him; and when he saw him, he was moved with pity. He went to him and bandaged his wounds, having poured oil and wine on them. Then he put him on his own animal, brought him to an inn, and took care of him. (Luke 10:30–34)

Jesus asked which of the three was a true neighbor to the injured man. "The one who showed him mercy," was the answer. Jesus then said, "Go and do likewise" (Luke 10:37).

There are many places in our world that we consider unsafe. Things were not all that different in Jesus's time. There were the areas to avoid such as the long, lonely roads in the Judean countryside filled with robbers and other troublemakers. Those who passed by the injured man, however, were worried about more than just their safety. They were concerned about their reputation as religious leaders, for touching a robbery victim might make them unclean. The Samaritan, on the other hand, never stopped to think about himself. He just did what needed to be done for a fellow human being in need. Instead of choosing indifference, he responded with empathy.

Come to the Quiet

Take some time to think about how the Good Samaritan's charitable actions might have positively influenced those around him. In addition to the effect on the man attacked by robbers, wouldn't it be interesting to know not only what the innkeeper thought, but whether the other guests were touched as well? Reflect also upon the positive mark left on the Good Samaritan's soul by his loving response.

Time for Self-Reflection

- In what ways might you need to take a different look at your life?
- How might your actions be inhibiting your true happiness as well as negatively affecting those around you?

—CONCLUSION—

Your Selfie Examination of Conscience

> God loves you right where you're at.
> But he also loves you too much to keep you there.
>
> —Anonymous

I am frequently asked to speak at Advent teas. These are popular gatherings for women's ministries at both Protestant and Catholic Churches. Often they involve one or two women hosting a table and inviting several of their friends to join them for an evening of faith and fellowship. The hope is that by allowing women a break from the usual hustle, bustle, and madness of the holidays, they will walk out of the event renewed and refreshed, having spent at least a few hours to actually reflect on the reason for the season.

Recently I developed a new presentation built around the beautiful examples given to us in the Blessed Mother; in particular, her *fiat* or "yes" to God. The title of the presentation is "Mary and the Three Rs: Reflect, Rejoice, Respond." How is it that such a young girl was able to respond so positively and quickly to the Lord's incredible invitation sent through St. Gabriel? Saying "yes" to being the "God bearer" would be life-altering in so many ways. Yet Mary, describing herself as a handmaid of the Lord, said, "Let it be done to me according to thy word."

She was able to respond so affirmatively because Mary was a young woman who reflected, contemplated, and "pondered."

We see her pondering things in her heart at the Presentation as well as the Finding of Jesus in the Temple. She was a woman of prayer who didn't just move from one activity to the next. She put her heart, mind, and soul, into everything she did, along with a lot of prayer.

But how many of us reflect or ponder anymore? Oh, maybe we take a few extra seconds to decide between the fish dinner or the special of the day at our favorite restaurant, but pondering and reflecting seem to be going the way of last year's fashions.

Now is your chance to dare to be different—to actually buck the trends of our frenetic world. You've already broken a norm by actually sitting down, reading this book, reviewing the selfie quizzes in each chapter, coming to the quiet, and engaging in self-reflection. Why not continue to blaze a new trail and go even deeper in attempt to break free of the selfie syndrome, which is all about the exterior and nothing about the interior. The four key questions below are designed to help you build on the big picture described in the previous chapter. The more time you take to explore spiritually probing questions, the stronger your relationship will be with God, as well as with those around you. You'll probably start to see an uptick on that happiness meter, too. Here are four important questions to consider:

1. Is God your copilot, and if so, are you willing to change seats? At first glance, the bumper sticker that reads "God is my copilot" might not sound so bad. But stop to think about it: Wouldn't the Alpha and the Omega, the Beginning and the End, the omnipotent One who created all things, the one who holds the entire universe in his hands, be who you want behind the wheel of your car—in the driver's seat? I mean, no matter how well you did on your driver's test, I think the Lord God Almighty would be a better bet to ensure your safety and the safety of those on the road. Isn't it a tad arrogant to think of the Lord of lords as an equal rather than in control not only of your car, but your life? This is another unfortunate fallout from our self-centered world. The typical attitude is, "Once in a while, if I need a second opinion, I'll throw up a prayer and see what sort of answers I get and whether they work for me. But otherwise, I've got this."

If you are a Christian, then you are called to love the Lord with all of your heart, mind, and strength. He is supposed to be front and center in your life—and yes, in the driver's seat. That doesn't mean you'll lose your free will. It also doesn't mean that you abandon all sense of structure in your life in terms of keeping certain schedules and making reasonable plans. It does mean, though, that you need to be sure your will is in line with God's will.

If you haven't made a commitment to Christ yet, what are you waiting for? There is no time like the present. If you're Catholic, you can start by going to confession and attending Mass regularly. If you are already meeting your weekly Mass obligations, that's great. Maybe you could spend some time before the Eucharist in Adoration. Perhaps it's time to enroll in that Bible study you've been thinking about. Or maybe the pregnancy resource center in your area needs more volunteers. During an address for a conference in Florence in November 2015, Pope Francis told his listeners that by putting others first, we're putting God first: "A Christian's humanity is not narcissistic or self-centered, but always goes out to others, which leads us always to work and to fight to make the world a better place."

2. Have you ever done what I call a "media reality check"? This is where you take some time to stop and really think about how your media consumption may be affecting your relationships with God and your family. We've already documented how easily people are influenced by the culture. The time you spend taking and posting selfies, surfing the web, and watching reality TV absolutely affects the way you see the world. Remember that great quote from Matthew Kelly? "The way people see the world is the way they live their lives."

The last time I checked, there wasn't an abundance of godly or even remotely wholesome content out there in media land, and this means that media consumers are seeing a very skewed view of the world—a world that has done a really good job of using the word "ego" as an acronym: Easing God Out. Be honest with God and yourself and think about how your media exposure may be affecting your attitude toward Church teachings; you know the ones I mean—those hot-button, not-very-PC, countercultural issues.

And what about your loved ones? In my first book *NOISE: How Our Media Saturated Culture Dominates Lives and Dismantles Families,* I open with a scene typical to most American families. The wife wakes up and goes into the bathroom to brush her teeth. The husband already has the radio blasting tuned to the local news-talk station. His cell phone is buzzing on the counter as he steps into the shower. She can hear the kids arguing over the remote. When she goes downstairs to make a quick breakfast before everyone rushes out the door, there is now silence. Two of her children are staring zombie-like at the TV. The other two don't even acknowledge her—they are busy texting their friends. She shrugs her shoulders and thinks, *If you can't beat 'em, join 'em.* She grabs her iPhone and starts checking her e-mail.

If this scene is even remotely familiar to you, it's time for that media reality check: an honest assessment of how much time you are spending with all things technology. Maybe it's time to do what former social media model Essena O'Neill suggests—take a week off of social media. If that makes you break out in hives or a cold sweat, at least have a general idea of how much time you spend with the media.

This is especially important if you have a spouse and children. Believe it or not, today's married couples only have about four minutes completely alone with each other each day. And children are like sponges, soaking up all of your examples and actions. So be cognizant of your own media habits.

3. Are you truly a child of God, or are you someone who sees herself as mostly autonomous and in control of her own destiny? This relates to the first question, but it provides some additional self-examination as to whether we are truly ready to let (in all deference to Carrie Underwood) "Jesus take the wheel."

It's not easy turning over the reins at first. However, the more you get to know God, the more you realize you are not—and never were—in control of anything in the first place. St. James reminds us beautifully of our foolishness when it comes to the control category.

> Come now, you who say, "Today or tomorrow we will go to such and such a town and spend a year there, doing business and making money..." Instead you

> ought to say, "If the Lord wishes, we will live and do this or that." (James 4:13, 15)

When I was growing up, my mother always used the phrase, "God spares," when referring to an upcoming event, such as a vacation or a road trip. "God spares, when we get back to New Jersey, we will spend some time with your cousins."

My mother-in-law used the phrase "God willing" in the same way when my husband was growing up. As children neither of us thought much about those words. However, much later, when we began to examine our own lives, we realized how wise both of our mothers were (and still are). We always thought, as hip, young urban professionals ready to take on the world after college graduation, that we had it all together. We were achieving our goals one after the other, marking off the items on our bucket lists, and we believed that our plans would always fall into place as long as we worked hard. The result would be, well, you know, walking off into the sunset and living happily ever after. We never thought that God had anything to do with it. Basically, somewhere in the back of our minds, we were grateful, but at the end of the day we took most of the credit.

There is nothing wrong with having goals and plans. The problems arise when we don't first see if those plans line up with what God has in mind for us. If they don't, we will never truly be happy.

> But strive first for the kingdom of God and his righteousness, and all these things will be given to you as well. (Matthew 6:33)

4. Are you willing to make some changes? We're all pilgrims on a journey. We're not home yet. All of us, no matter how faithful, are called to daily conversion. Jesus promises us that he has come so our joy will be complete (see John 15:11).

Since we are sojourners our joy won't be totally complete until we are united with Jesus in heaven. That doesn't mean that we're doomed to a life of total misery and suffering during our time on planet earth, though. It does mean that joy is different than temporary happiness. We will all have our down times during this lifetime. It's not a matter of if, but when. But true joy isn't shaken by momentary troubles. Think of the word *joy* as another acronym: Jesus first, Others second, Yourself last.

In the back of this book you will find a list of websites, Bible studies, and other resources, organizations, and activities that can help you move closer to God and further away from our self-absorbed world. There are plenty of steps we can take to help us move in the right direction. Maybe it can start with taking fewer selfies, using the time it would take to post those selfies to instead read a Bible passage, say a prayer, or finally offer to help that elderly neighbor clean up the backyard. It could mean turning off your favorite reality TV program and spend that time reading a book that will help you grow spiritually. You might choose to attend Mass during the week in addition to the Sunday obligation. On the way out of church, grab a copy of the bulletin and see how you could be of service to your pastor and the parish, whether it's joining a committee or participating in a Bible study or prayer group.

This journey of my own "selfie discovery" began with the story of tracing my roots—my husband and I reconnecting with our ethnic and Catholic heritage in Italy. So it is fitting to close this portion of the pilgrim journey with more words of wisdom from Pope Francis on the importance of never forgetting where we came from. We are all called to be more selfless instead of selfish because we are a Church, the pope says, that doesn't live in isolation, closed in on itself. It's a Church among the people and for the people.

> A disciple must maintain a healthy contact with reality and with people's lives with their joys and sorrows... [this] is the only way to be able to help and communicate with them. [Christ's disciples] should never forget from where they have been chosen, namely from among the people, and must never fall into the temptation of adopting an aloof or detached attitude as if the thoughts and lives of the people were not their concern and of no importance for them. The Church, like Jesus, lives among the people and for the people.[77]

Nurturing a personal faith in Jesus enables us to see the truth of our human condition and add our contribution "to the full humanization of society"—and experience joy and lasting happiness as well. Enjoy the journey!

—APPENDIX A—

The Ultimate "Selfie Syndrome" Resources List

Tools to Help You and Your Family Be Less Selfie-Centered

It's a great time to be Catholic. We have so many solid resources to help us grow, including books and CDs, conferences, DVD series, Scripture studies, and Catholic media outlets! The following resource list is meant to be user-friendly. You don't need a theology degree or any type of religious studies background to get started. All you need is an open heart and a sincere interest in growing closer to Christ. The tools, websites, and suggested books cover a variety of topics and activities. How do I know? I use many of them myself. These are the tools that I recommend regularly to my listeners, Facebook followers, and conference attendees. So let's get started.

Read the Scriptures!

Not too long ago I was giving a women's retreat and I mentioned the importance of being in God's Word every day. During the question-and-answer period, a young woman raised her hand, looking somewhat perplexed.

"I really want to study God's Word, but I have never even cracked open a Bible," she said. "Is that what I do? Just open the Bible and start reading?"

Certainly that's one option. But given all the great resources available along with the confusion that can occur without proper interpretation, if it's your first attempt at Bible study, it's best not to go it alone. Besides, it's a lot more fun, interesting, and educational to talk with other people about a particular Gospel passage or Scripture verse that may have impacted their life or yours.

We are blessed in the Catholic Church, which is the universal Church, to be in unison with all other Catholics across the globe thanks to the established liturgical calendar and the daily Mass readings.

If diving into a Bible study class is too much for you to tackle right now, a good place to begin is to start following the daily readings in a daily Catholic devotional. Devotionals include a reflection for each day to help you apply the reading to your daily life. It's an easy, non-threatening way to get started, regardless of how much or how little you know about Scripture. (But don't be afraid to give Bible study a try as well. Most meet once a week and include a video or DVD presentation in addition to a discussion of the study questions.)

Catholic Devotionals

Living Faith (www.livingfaith.com)
Magnificat (www.magnificat.com)
Word Among Us (www.wau.org)

Bible Studies

Catholic Scripture Study (www.cssprogram.net)
Full of Grace: The Women of Grace Foundational Study Series (www.womenofgrace.com)
Great Adventure Catholic Bible Study (www.biblestudyforcatholics.com)

Programs and Websites

Archbishop Fulton Sheen said, "There are not one hundred people in the United States that hate the Church, but there are millions who hate what they wrongly perceive the Church to be." Many of those are Catholics who were poorly catechized and left the faith.

I myself was one of those poorly catechized Catholics. Although I didn't hate the Church, I certainly didn't really know the beauty of her teachings. The good news is that there are a wide variety of programs designed to help Catholics embrace the faith. The programs listed below cover a variety of areas within the Church including Church history, sacraments, prayer, evangelization, and marriage enrichment.

The Alexander House (www.alexanderhouse.org). Ministry for troubled marriages

Beloved (www.lighthousecatholicmedia/beloved.org). DVD series on the mystery and the meaning of marriage

Christlife Catholic Ministry for Evangelization (www.christlife.org)

Couple Prayer (www.coupleprayer.org). Group/home study encouraging and teaching couples to pray together

Footprints of God (www.ignatius.com). DVD series on salvation history

ENDOW Catholic Women's Studies (www.endowgroups.org)

Symbolon (www.symboloncatholic.org). Faith-formation DVD series for the parish

WINE (Women in the New Evangelization) Study Groups. (womeninthenewevangelization.com)

Catholic Media

Would you like to know what the pope *actually* said and did versus what the media say he said and did? Tune into Catholic radio or TV, or pick up one of the many solid Catholic publications now available. Catholic radio and TV are dedicated to explaining and teaching the faith through dynamic and engaging programs. With 24/7 Catholic talk radio and 24/7 Catholic television, what are you waiting for?

Despite the fact that Catholic media have exploded over the past twenty years—EWTN Global Catholic Radio, for example, now has more than three hundred radio affiliates around the country and close to five hundred around the world, not to mention our presence on satellite radio—we still have a long way to go to be heard among all the other voices out there competing for the public's attention. So tune in and help us spread the word.

EWTN Global Catholic Radio/TV (www.ewtn.com)
Ave Maria Radio (www.avemariaradio.net)
First Things (www.firstthings.com)
The Catholic Channel (www.siriusxm.com/thecatholicchannel)
National Catholic Register (www.ncregister.com)
Our Sunday Visitor (www.osv.com)

—NOTES—

1. Antonia Malloy, "'Selfie obsessed' teenager Danny Bowman suicidal after failing to capture 'the perfect selfie,'" *Independent News Service*, March 28, 2014. http://www.independent.co.uk/news/uk/home-news/selfie-obsession-made-teenager-danny-bowman-suicidal-9212421.html.
2. Terry Goodrich, "Cellphone Addiction is an Increasingly Realistic Possibility: Baylor Study of College Students Reveals," *Journal of Behavior Addictions,* August 27, 2014. http://www.baylor.edu/mediacommunications/news.php?action=story&story=145864.
3. Goodrich.
4. Pope Benedict XVI, Forty-Fifth World Communications Day Message, "Truth, Proclamation, and Authenticity of Life in the Digital Age," June 5, 2011. http://w2.vatican.va/content/benedict-xvi/en/messages/communications/documents/hf_ben-xvi_mes_20110124_45th-world-communications-day.html.
5. Pope Benedict XVI, Forty-Fifth World Communications Day Message.
6. "Dark for Dinner" as part of the Georgia-Pacific Dixie Brand "Be More Here" campaign. http://www.dixie.com/bemorehere.
7. Pope Francis, Message of Pope Francis for the Forty-Eighth World Communications Day, "Communication at the Service of an Authentic Culture of Encounter," June 1, 2014. https://w2.vatican.va/content/francesco/en/messages/communications/documents/papa-francesco_20140124_messaggio-comunicazioni-sociali.html.
8. Lucy Larcom, ed. *The Life and Letters of Madame Swetchine,* 6th edition, trans. H.W. Preston (Cambridge, MA: Roberts Brothers, 1869), 14.
9. Joseph Pimentel, "Disney California Adventure roller coaster halted after person pulls out selfie stick," *The Orange County Register*, June 24, 2015. http://www.ocregister.com/articles/selfie-668467-stick-ride.html.
10. Malloy.

11. Deborah Hastings, "Woman in North Carolina killed while driving and texting about being 'happy,'" *New York Daily News*, April 26, 2014. http://www.nydailynews.com/news/national/north-carolina-woman-dies-behind-wheel-texting-happy-article-1.1769965.
12. Chris Perez, "Tourist plunges to her death while taking selfie," *New York Post,* November 5, 2014. http://nypost.com/2014/11/05/tourist-plunges-to-her-death-while-taking-selfie/.
13. Hannah Roberts, "Italian girl plunges 60ft to her death as she attempted to take a selfie while on jagged rocks in the seaside town of Taranto," *Daily Mail*, June 12, 2014; http://www.dailymail.co.uk/news/article-2656419/Italian-girl-plunges-60ft-death-attempted-selfie-jagged-rocks-seaside-town-Taranto.html.
14. "2014 Will Go Down as the Year of the Death Selfie." http://www.brobible.com/life/article/death-selfie-2014; December 12, 2014.
15. Cailey Rizzo, "More people have died from selfies than shark attacks this year," Mashable, September 21, 2015; http://www.newsjs.com/url.php?p=http://mashable.com/2015/09/21/selfie-deaths/.
16. Brian Daly, "Russian government launches a 'safe selfie' campaign," *Fortune Magazine*, July 9, 2015; http://fortune.com/2015/07/09/russia-safe-selfie-campaign/
17. "SELFIE is named Oxford Dictionaries Word of the Year 2013," Oxford Word Blog, Oxford University Press, November 19, 2013.
18. Abhijeet Mishra, "1 billion 30-day active Android users, 93 million selfies taken each day," *Android Beat*, June 25, 2014. http://www.androidbeat.com/2014/06/1-billion-30-day-active-android-users-93-million-selfies-taken-day/.
19. Pew Research Center, "More Than Half of Millennials Have Shared a 'Selfie,'" March 4, 2014; http://www.pewresearch.org/fact-tank/2014/03/04/more-than-half-of-Millennials-have-shared-a-selfie.
20. Pamela Rutledge, Ph.D., M.B.A., "Making Sense of Selfies: Taking selfies feels problematic because we aren't used to them,"

Psychology Today, July 6, 2013. https://www.psychologytoday.com/blog/positively-media/201307/making-sense-selfies.

21. Teresa of Avila, *Interior Castle,* ed. and trans. E. Allison Peers (Mineola, NY: Dover, 1946), 23.
22. Teresa of Avila, *The Collected Works of Saint Teresa of Avila,* trans. Kieran Kavanaugh, O.C.D., and Otilio Rodriguez, O.C.D. (Washington, DC: ICS, 1985), 3.12.7.
23. Shawna Malcom, "Up in Kim Kardashian's Business," *Cosmopolitan,* October 2, 2009; http://www.cosmopolitan.com/entertainment/celebs/news/a2990/kim-kardashian-1109/.
24. Stephanie Marcus, "Kim Kardashian Named One of TIME Magazine's 30 Most Influential People on the Internet," *Huffington Post, Huff Post Entertainment*, March 5, 2015. http://www.huffingtonpost.com/2015/03/06/kim-kardashian-most-influential-internet_n_6818940.html.
25. Alison Flood, "Kim Kardashian's Booked Snapped Up by Thousands," *The Guardian*, May 18, 2015. http://www.theguardian.com/books/2015/may/18/kim-kardashian-selfish-book-selfies.
26. Pepper Schwartz, "Kim Kardashian: Queen of Narcissism," *CNN Opinion,* August 18, 2014. http://www.cnn.com/2014/08/13/opinion/schwartz-kim-k-selfies/index.html.
27. Schwartz.
28. Maria Konnikova, "How Facebook Makes Us Unhappy," *The New Yorker*, September 10, 2013. http://www.newyorker.com/tech/elements/how-facebook-makes-us-unhappy.
29. Belinda Goldsmith, "Is Facebook Envy Making You Miserable?" *Reuters,* January 22, 2013. http://uk.reuters.com/article/2013/01/22/us-facebook-envy-idUKBRE90L0N220130122.
30. Pope Benedict XVI, Forty-Seventh World Communications Day Statement; "Social Networks Portals of Truth and New: New Spaces for Evangelization"; May 12, 2013; http://w2.vatican.va/content/benedict-xvi/en/messages/communications/documents/hf_ben-xvi_mes_20130124_47th-world-communications-day.html. Emphasis added.

31. Fr. Pedro Arrupe, S.J., "Fall in Love: A Poem," *Finding God in All Things: A Marquette Prayer Book* (Milwaukee: Marquette University Press, 2009), 98. As quoted on *Ignatian Spirituality* website, http://www.ignatianspirituality.com/ignatian-prayer/prayers-by-st-ignatius-and-others/fall-in-love.
32. Pope John Paul II, World Youth Day, Prayer Vigil Address in Denver, Colorado, August 19, 2000; https://w2.vatican.va/content/john-paul-ii/en/speeches/2000/jul-sep/documents/hf_jp-ii_spe_20000819_gmg-veglia.html.
33. James Allen, "The Finding of a Principle," *Mind Is the Master: The Complete James Allen Treasury* (New York: Penguin, 2010).
34. Jeff Grabmeier, "Hey, Guys: Posting a Lot of Selfies Doesn't Send a Good Message: Posting more online photos of yourself may suggest anti-social traits," Ohio State University, January 6, 2015, https://news.osu.edu/news/2015/01/06/hey-guys-posting-a-lot-of-selfies-doesn%E2%80%99t-send-a-good-message/cite.
35. F.K. Bartels, "The Most Holy Trinity: Supreme Model for Family and Marriage," *Catholic Online*, July 2, 2010. http://www.catholic.org/news/hf/family/story.php?id=37200.
36. Fr. Robert Spitzer, S.J., Ph.D., *The Soul's Upward Yearning: Clues to our Transcendent From Nature and Reason* (San Francisco: Ignatius, 2015), 15–16.
37. Spitzer, 15–16.
38. "U.S. Public Becoming Less Religious," 2014 Religious Landscape Study, Pew Forum on Religious and Public Life, November 3, 2015. http://www.pewforum.org/2015/11/03/u-s-public-becoming-less-religious/.
39. Blessed Pier Giorgio Frassati, "Novena in Honor of Blessed Frassati," Day 8, Frassati USA. http://frassatiusa.org/eighth-day.
40. Anthony Horowitz, "L. Frank Baum: The Real Wizard of Oz," *Telegraph,* February 10, 2016. http://www.telegraph.co.uk/culture/5949617/L-Frank-Baum-the-real-Wizard-of-Oz.html.
41. Sue Ellen Browder, interview with author for *Catholic Connections,* October 26, 2015.

42. Browder, interview with author for *Catholic Connections.*
43. Browder, interview with author for *Catholic Connections.*
44. Fr. Paul Check, Courage, Living the Truth in Love Conference, Pontifical University of St. Thomas, Rome, Italy, October 2, 2015.
45. Fr. Paul Check, Courage, Living the Truth in Love Conference.
46. Fr. Paul Check, "Love One Another as I Have Loved You" at the Courage Conference, Detroit, Michigan, August 10, 2015.
47. Vatican International Theological Commission, *Communion and Stewardship: Human Persons Created in the Image of God,* 25. http://www.vatican.va/roman_curia/congregations/cfaith/cti_documents/rc_con_cfaith_doc_20040723_communion-stewardship_en.html.
48. Fr. Paul Check, "Love One Another."
49. Greg Botelho, "Ex-NAACP leader Rachel Dolezal: 'I identify as black,'" CNN, June 17, 2015. http://www.cnn.com/2015/06/16/us/washington-rachel-dolezal-naacp/.
50. Pope Francis, Twenty-Eighth World Youth Day Address to Community of Varginha, Brazil, July 23, 2013. https://w2.vatican.va/content/francesco/en/speeches/2013/july/documents/papa-francesco_20130725_gmg-comunita-varginha.html.
51. Sue Ellen Browder, *Subverted: How I Helped the Sexual Revolution Hijack the Women's Movement* (San Francisco: Ignatius, 2015), 37.
52. Helen Gurley Brown, *Sex and The Single Girl* (Fort Lee, NJ: Barricade, 2003), 15.
53. Browder, *Subverted*, 33–34.
54. American Academy of Facial Plastic and Reconstructive Surgery (AFPRS), *Annual AAFPRS Survey Finds 'Selfie' Trend Increases Demand for Facial Plastic Surgery Influence on Elective Surgery*, March 11, 2014. http://www.aafprs.org/media/press_release/20140311.html.
55. Sarah Rainey, "Secretly Starving: Inside the Virtual World of Anorexia Blogging," *Telegraph,* February 25, 2014. https://a248.e.akamai.net/f/1362/5848/6m/s.telegraph.co.uk/graphics/projects/inside-the-world-of-anorexia-blogging/.

56. Gary L. Schreiber and Lisa Stanley, "Susan Dey's Anorexia," *Woman's Day,* May 20, 1993, 8.
57. Wade, Keski-Rahkonen, and Hudson, "Get the Facts on Eating Disorders," National Eating Disorders Association, 2011. https://www.nationaleatingdisorders.org/get-facts-eating-disorders.
58. Jean Kilbourne interview with Cindy Crawford, "Killing Us Softly 4: Advertising's Image of Women," Definatalie.com, March 12, 2010. http://www.definatalie.com/killing-us-softly-4/.
59. Catholic News Agency/EWTN News, "Pope Gives Surprising Inflight Press Conference," July 29, 2013. http://www.catholicnewsagency.com/news/pope-gives-surprising-in-flight-press-conference/.
60. Archbishop Charles J. Chaput, "Public Witness and Faithful Citizensh*ip,*" *Catholic Philly*, October 18, 2012. http://catholicphilly.com/2012/10/think-tank/weekly-message-from-archbishop-chaput/public-witness-and-catholic-citizenship/.
61. Lauren Markoe, "Pew study: More Americans reject religion, but believers firm in faith," Religion News Service, November 3, 2015. http://www.religionnews.com/2015/11/03/pew-americans-religion-believers-faith/.
62. Jonah Bromwich, "Essena O'Neill, Instagram Star Recaptures Her Life," *The New York Times*, November 3, 2015. http://www.nytimes.com/2015/11/04/fashion/essena-oneill-instagram-star-recaptions-her-life.html?src=mv&_r=0.
63. Elle Hunt, "Essena O'Neill quits Instagram claiming social media 'is not real life,'" *The Guardian*, November 3, 2015. http://www.theguardian.com/media/2015/nov/03/instagram-star-essena-oneill-quits-2d-life-to-reveal-true-story-behind-images.
64. Essenna O'Neill's website: www.letsbegamechangers.com.
65. O'Neill, www.letsbegamechangers.com.
66. O'Neill, www.letsbegamechangers.com.
67. Pope Francis, as quoted by Elise Harris, "Pope: If you don't serve others, then what are you living for?" Catholic News Agency, November 3, 2015.
68. Pope Francis, "Pope: If you don't serve others, then what are you living for?"

69. *Sunset Boulevard*, Billy Wilder, Paramount Pictures, 1950.
70. Sam Kashner, "Both Huntress and Prey," *Vanity Fair*, October 20, 2014. http://www.vanityfair.com/hollywood/2014/10/jennifer-lawrence-photo-hacking-privacy.
71. Kashner.
72. Melissa Henson, "5 Media Resolutions for The New Year," Parents Television Council, January 4, 2016. http://w2.parentstv.org/blog/index.php/2016/01/04/5-media-resolutions-for-the-new-year/.
73. Pope Benedict XVI, Forty-Fifth World Communications Day Statement; "Truth, Proclamation, and Authenticity of Life in the Digital Age," June 5, 2011. http://w2.vatican.va/content/benedict-xvi/en/messages/communications/documents/hf_ben-xvi_mes_20110124_45th-world-communications-day.html.
74. Bradley W. Wilcox, "Strong families, prosperous states: Do healthy families affect the wealth of states?" American Enterprise Institute, October 19, 2015. https://www.aei.org/press/do-healthy-families-affect-the-wealth-of-states/.
75. Everett Rosenfeld, "Social networking linked to divorce, marital unhappiness." CNBC, July 8, 2014. http://www.cnbc.com/2014/07/08/.
76. Bishop Paul S. Loverde, *Bought with a Price: Every Man's Duty to Protect Himself and His Family from a Pornographic Culture* (Arlington, VA: Catholic Diocese of Arlington, 2014), 15.
77. Pope Francis on Vatican Radio, "Pope: The Church lives among the people and for the people," November 10, 2015. http://en.radiovaticana.va/news/2015/11/10/pope_the_church_lives_among_the_people_and_for_the_people/1185761.